$1K Payday: A Journey to Financial Freedom in 2024

Dedication

To my beautiful wife, Katerina, and my son, Thalis, whose love and support inspire me every day.

About Me

Hello, I'm Demetris Papadopoulos, an entrepreneur with a passion for helping others achieve financial independence. My journey has been one of relentless pursuit of knowledge and growth. I've explored various avenues of income generation, from freelancing and digital product creation to e-commerce and real estate crowdfunding. My mission is to share these insights with you, empowering you to achieve your financial goals. You can learn more about my work and ventures at d-papa.com and Limitless Passion Ltd.

I0466944

Table of Contents

Introduction: Embracing the Gig Economy

Welcome to the dynamic world of the gig economy, where opportunities for generating income are as diverse as they are abundant. The traditional employment landscape has been revolutionized, offering unprecedented flexibility and the ability to earn through various side hustles and freelance work.

 The gig economy thrives on technological advancements and the evolving needs of the modern workforce, allowing you to create a sustainable income on your own terms.

Let's explore the strategies that can empower you to achieve financial freedom in 2024.

Chapter 1: Freelancing Essentials

Welcome to the exciting world of freelancing, where your skills and passion can lead to substantial financial rewards. In 2024, freelancing continues to be a dominant force in the gig economy, offering unparalleled flexibility and the potential for significant income. Whether you're a seasoned professional or just starting, this chapter will guide you through the essentials of freelancing, from identifying marketable skills to navigating platforms and building a successful profile.

Discovering Marketable Skills

The foundation of a successful freelancing career lies in recognizing and honing your marketable skills. These are the abilities that clients are willing to pay for, and they can range widely depending on your expertise and interests. Here's how to identify and leverage your skills for maximum impact:

1. **Self-Assessment**: Begin by conducting a thorough self-assessment. List out your skills, experiences, and areas of expertise. Consider both hard skills (technical abilities) and soft skills (communication, problem-solving). Tools like

LinkedIn's skill assessments or online quizzes can provide insights into your strengths.

2. **Market Research**: Once you've identified your skills, research the market demand for them. Platforms like Upwork, Freelancer, and Fiverr have sections where you can see the most in-demand skills and the average rates for those services. This will help you understand where your skills fit in and how to price them competitively.

3. **Skill Enhancement**: If you find gaps between your current skill set and market demand, invest time in learning and improving. Online courses from platforms like Coursera, Udemy, or Skillshare can help you acquire new skills or enhance existing ones. Certifications in specific areas can also boost your credibility and attract more clients.

Platforms for Freelance Work

With your marketable skills identified, the next step is to find the right platforms to offer your services. Each platform has its own strengths, and choosing the right one can make a significant difference in your freelancing success.

1. **Upwork**: One of the largest freelancing platforms, Upwork offers opportunities across a wide range of industries. It's suitable for both beginners and experienced freelancers. The platform provides tools to create detailed profiles, bid on projects, and manage contracts. Upwork's escrow system ensures secure payments, making it a reliable choice.

2. **Freelancer**: Similar to Upwork, Freelancer allows you to compete for projects by submitting bids. It covers a wide array of categories, from writing and design to programming and marketing. Freelancer also offers contests where you can showcase your skills and win projects based on your submissions.

3. **Fiverr**: Known for its "gig" system, Fiverr lets freelancers list services starting at $5. This platform is ideal for creative and digital services like graphic design, writing, and video editing.

Fiverr's structure allows you to create packages and add-ons, giving clients flexible options and increasing your earning potential.

4. **Specialized Platforms**: Depending on your niche, there are platforms that cater specifically to certain fields. For instance, Toptal connects top-tier freelancers with clients in tech and finance, while Contently is great for writers and journalists. These platforms often have rigorous vetting processes but can offer higher-paying opportunities.

Building a Successful Freelance Profile

Your profile is your digital storefront—it's often the first impression potential clients will have of you. A well-crafted profile can set you apart from the competition and attract high-quality clients. Here's how to build an engaging and professional profile:

1. **Professional Photo**: A clear, professional headshot can significantly impact client perception. Make sure your photo is high-quality, with good lighting and a neutral background. Dress appropriately to reflect your professional persona.

2. **Compelling Bio**: Your bio should be concise, engaging, and focused on what you can offer clients. Highlight your expertise, experience, and any unique qualities that set you apart. Use keywords relevant to your industry to improve your profile's visibility in searches.

3. **Detailed Portfolio**: Showcase your best work through a well-organized portfolio. Include a variety of samples that demonstrate your range and capabilities. For writers, this could be articles and blog posts; for designers, a collection of logos, web designs, or illustrations. Always seek permission before including client work.

4. **Testimonials and Reviews**: Positive feedback from previous clients can build trust and credibility. If you're just starting, consider offering services at a discounted rate or even for free to gather testimonials. Highlight these reviews prominently on your profile.

5. **Skill Tests and Certifications**: Many platforms offer skill tests that can validate your expertise. Completing these tests can enhance your profile and give clients confidence in your abilities. Additionally, include any relevant certifications or training courses you've completed.

6. **Clear and Professional Communication**: Your communication style reflects your professionalism. Ensure that your profile is free from grammatical errors and clearly communicates your services. Respond promptly to client inquiries and maintain a courteous and professional tone.

Setting Your Rates and Managing Finances

Determining your rates and managing your finances effectively are crucial aspects of freelancing. Here's how to set competitive rates and keep your finances in check:

1. **Research and Benchmarking**: Start by researching the average rates for your services on various platforms. Consider factors like your experience, the complexity of the work, and industry standards. Websites like Glassdoor and Payscale can provide insights into typical freelance rates.

2. **Pricing Strategies**: Choose a pricing strategy that works for you. Hourly rates are common for ongoing projects, while fixed rates are suitable for specific tasks or projects. You can also offer package deals on platforms like Fiverr, combining multiple services at a discounted rate.

3. **Value-Based Pricing**: Consider value-based pricing, where you set rates based on the value you provide to the client rather than just the hours worked. This approach can be particularly effective for projects that significantly impact a client's business, like a website redesign or a comprehensive marketing strategy.

4. **Financial Management**: As a freelancer, you're responsible for managing your own finances, including taxes. Use tools like QuickBooks or FreshBooks to track your income, expenses, and invoices. Set aside a portion of your earnings for

taxes, and consider consulting with a financial advisor or accountant to ensure you're meeting your tax obligations.

5. **Contracts and Agreements**: Always use contracts to outline the scope of work, payment terms, deadlines, and other important details. This protects both you and the client and helps prevent misunderstandings. Many freelancing platforms offer contract templates you can customize for your projects.

Finding and Securing Freelance Projects

Finding and securing projects is a continuous process that requires strategic effort. Here are some tips to help you consistently land freelance work:

1. **Networking**: Leverage your professional network to find freelance opportunities. Attend industry events, join online forums, and participate in community groups related to your field. Networking can lead to referrals and repeat business from satisfied clients.

2. **Proposals and Pitches**: Crafting compelling proposals is key to winning projects. Tailor each proposal to the specific client and project, highlighting how your skills and experience make you the perfect fit. Be clear about your proposed solution, timeline, and pricing.

3. **Building Relationships**: Focus on building long-term relationships with clients rather than just completing one-off projects. Consistent, high-quality work can lead to repeat business and referrals. Communicate regularly, deliver on time, and exceed client expectations to foster strong relationships.

4. **Marketing Yourself**: Treat your freelancing career as a business and invest in marketing yourself. Create a professional website showcasing your portfolio, services, and client testimonials. Use social media to share your work, engage with potential clients, and establish yourself as an expert in your field.

5. **Staying Active on Platforms**: Regularly update your profiles on freelancing platforms and stay active by bidding on new projects. Many platforms reward active users by boosting their visibility in search results. Respond quickly to job postings and follow up on proposals to demonstrate your enthusiasm and reliability.

Managing Freelance Projects

Efficient project management is crucial to delivering quality work on time and maintaining client satisfaction. Here's how to manage your freelance projects effectively:

1. **Project Planning**: Start each project with a clear plan. Break down the project into manageable tasks, set deadlines for each task, and prioritize based on importance and deadlines. Use project management tools like Trello, Asana, or Monday.com to keep track of your tasks and deadlines.

2. **Time Management**: Effective time management ensures you meet deadlines without compromising quality. Use time-tracking tools like Toggl or Harvest to monitor how much time you spend on each task. Allocate specific times for focused work, breaks, and administrative tasks.

3. **Communication**: Maintain clear and consistent communication with your clients. Provide regular updates on project progress, discuss any potential issues early, and seek feedback to ensure you're meeting their expectations. Good communication builds trust and reduces the risk of misunderstandings.

4. **Quality Assurance**: Before submitting your work, review it thoroughly to ensure it meets the client's requirements and your quality standards. Proofread documents, test software, and double-check designs to catch any errors. Delivering high-quality work consistently can lead to repeat business and positive reviews.

5. **Handling Revisions**: Revisions are a common part of freelancing. Approach them professionally and use feedback to

improve your work. Set clear boundaries on the number of revisions included in your initial price and charge accordingly for additional changes. This ensures that both you and the client have a clear understanding of the scope of work.

Building a Sustainable Freelance Career

Building a sustainable freelance career requires more than just securing projects; it involves continuous learning, adaptation, and strategic planning. Here are some strategies to ensure long-term success:

1. **Continuous Learning**: The freelance market is dynamic, with new tools, technologies, and trends emerging regularly. Invest in continuous learning to stay ahead. Take online courses, attend workshops, and read industry publications to keep your skills relevant and competitive.

2. **Diversifying Income Streams**: Relying on a single income source can be risky. Diversify your income by offering various services, exploring multiple platforms, and developing passive income streams like digital products or online courses. This reduces financial instability and opens up new opportunities.

3. **Building a Personal Brand**: Establish a strong personal brand that reflects your expertise and values. Consistently deliver high-quality work, engage with your audience on social media, and contribute to industry discussions. A strong personal brand can attract high-paying clients and create more opportunities.

4. **Managing Work-Life Balance**: Freelancing offers flexibility, but it can also blur the lines between work and personal life. Set clear boundaries, create a dedicated workspace, and establish a routine that includes time for rest and personal activities. Maintaining a healthy work-life balance is essential for long-term productivity and well-being.

5. **Scaling Your Business**: As your freelance career grows, consider scaling your business. This could involve hiring subcontractors to handle excess work, expanding your service offerings, or increasing your rates as your expertise grows.

Scaling allows you to take on more clients and increase your income without overextending yourself.

Overcoming Challenges in Freelancing

Freelancing comes with its own set of challenges, from finding consistent work to managing client expectations. Here's how to overcome some common obstacles:

1. **Finding Consistent Work**: To maintain a steady flow of projects, diversify your client base and continually market yourself. Stay active on multiple freelancing platforms, network regularly, and ask satisfied clients for referrals and testimonials.

2. **Managing Client Expectations**: Clear communication is key to managing client expectations. Set realistic deadlines, outline the scope of work in contracts, and provide regular updates. If a project scope changes, discuss the implications with the client and adjust timelines and pricing accordingly.

3. **Dealing with Difficult Clients**: Not all client relationships will be smooth. Handle difficult clients professionally by listening to their concerns, addressing issues promptly, and maintaining a positive attitude. If a client relationship becomes untenable, know when to part ways amicably.

4. **Avoiding Burnout**: Freelancing can be demanding, leading to burnout if not managed well. Take regular breaks, prioritize self-care, and avoid overcommitting. Learn to say no to projects that don't align with your goals or capacity.

5. **Financial Uncertainty**: Freelancers often face fluctuating income. Create a financial buffer by saving a portion of your earnings and diversifying your income streams. Consider taking on retainer clients who provide consistent monthly income.

Future Trends in Freelancing

Staying ahead of future trends can give you a competitive edge. Here are some trends to watch in the freelancing world:

1. **Remote Work**: The shift towards remote work is likely to continue, increasing demand for freelancers. This trend offers opportunities to work with clients globally, expanding your market.

2. **Specialization**: Clients increasingly seek specialized skills. Position yourself as an expert in a niche area to attract higher-paying projects and stand out from the competition.

3. **Technology Integration**: Emerging technologies like AI, blockchain, and AR/VR are creating new opportunities for freelancers. Stay updated on these technologies and consider how they can be integrated into your services.

4. **Sustainable Freelancing**: There's growing awareness around sustainability and ethical practices. Freelancers who align their services with these values can attract clients who prioritize corporate social responsibility.

5. **Collaborative Platforms**: New platforms are emerging that focus on collaborative projects, connecting freelancers with teams and larger organizations. These platforms can offer opportunities for more substantial and complex projects.

By understanding the fundamentals of freelancing and continuously adapting to new trends, you can build a sustainable and rewarding freelance career.

The key to success lies in identifying your strengths, leveraging the right platforms, and delivering consistent, high-quality work.

With dedication, strategic planning, and a proactive approach, achieving a monthly income of $1,000 or more is well within your reach.

Chapter 2: Digital Product Creation

Welcome to the fascinating world of digital product creation, where the only limit is your imagination. In 2024, the digital marketplace offers unparalleled opportunities for generating income with minimal overhead. From ebooks and online courses to software, graphic designs, stock photography, and music, digital products can be created and sold to a global audience. Let's dive into how you can leverage these opportunities to build a steady stream of income.

The Spectrum of Digital Products

Digital products are unique in that they require no physical materials to produce and can be replicated infinitely at no additional cost. Here are some popular types of digital products you can create:

1. **Ebooks and Guides**: If you have expertise in a particular field, you can compile your knowledge into a comprehensive guide or instructional ebook. These are among the most straightforward digital products to create and sell.

2. **Online Courses and Webinars**: E-learning is booming, and creating digital courses or webinars allows you to teach skills and share knowledge across various subjects, from cooking and fitness to programming and business management.

3. **Software and Apps**: For those with technical skills, developing software, mobile apps, or web-based tools can be highly profitable. These range from simple productivity tools to complex enterprise software.

4. **Graphic Designs and Templates**: There is a continuous demand for digital graphics, including website themes, PowerPoint templates, and social media post designs.

5. **Stock Photography and Video**: Photographers and videographers can sell their media to stock photo websites or directly to clients who need high-quality images and footage for commercial use.

6. **Music and Audio Products**: Musicians and audio engineers can produce and sell beats, songs, sound effects, and audiobooks.

Tools for Creation and Distribution

To successfully create and sell digital products, you need the right tools. Here are some essential tools for various types of digital products:

1. **Product Creation Tools**: Depending on the type of digital product, various tools are required. For ebooks, software like Adobe InDesign or free tools like Canva work well. For courses, video recording software like Camtasia or ScreenFlow can be used. Software development requires coding tools and environments specific to the programming language used.

2. **Distribution Platforms**: Choosing the right platform to sell your products is crucial. Here are some platforms that can help you reach a wide audience:

   - **Gumroad**: Ideal for selling ebooks, courses, and other digital products. It handles payments and delivery, making it easy to get started.
   - **Teachable**: A popular platform for creating and selling online courses. It offers robust features for course creation, marketing, and student management.
   - **WarriorPlus and JVZoo**: These platforms are excellent for digital marketers and product creators. They offer features for affiliate marketing, allowing you to leverage a network of affiliates to sell your products.
   - **PassionFuze**: As part of my own offerings, PassionFuze teaches you how to create, launch, and sell digital products effectively. It's a comprehensive resource for anyone looking to dive into digital product creation.

Creating Your Digital Product

Creating a high-quality digital product involves several steps, from planning and content creation to finalizing and packaging your product. Here's a detailed guide to help you through the process:

1. **Idea Validation**: Before you start creating, validate your idea. Conduct market research to ensure there's a demand for your product. Look at competitors, target audience needs, and market trends. Use tools like Google Trends, keyword research tools, and surveys to gather data.

2. **Planning and Outlining**: Once your idea is validated, create a detailed plan. Outline the content, structure, and key points you want to cover. For ebooks, this might include chapters and sections; for courses, it could be modules and lessons.

3. **Content Creation**: Start creating your content based on your outline. Use tools that suit your product type:

   o **Ebooks**: Write your content using word processors like Microsoft Word or Google Docs. Use Canva or Adobe InDesign for design and layout.
   o **Courses**: Record video lessons using tools like Camtasia or ScreenFlow. Create supporting materials like PDFs, quizzes, and assignments.
   o **Software**: Develop your software using appropriate coding environments and test it thoroughly for bugs and usability issues.
   o **Graphic Designs**: Use design software like Adobe Illustrator, Photoshop, or free tools like Canva.

4. **Editing and Proofreading**: Review your content for errors and inconsistencies. For written content, consider hiring a professional editor. For video content, ensure the audio and visual quality are top-notch.

5. **Finalizing and Packaging**: Package your product in a user-friendly format. For ebooks, export them as PDFs or ePub files. For courses, upload the videos and materials to your chosen platform. For software, ensure it's easy to install and use.

Marketing Your Digital Products

Creating a great product is only half the battle; effective marketing is crucial to reach your target audience and generate sales. Here are some key marketing strategies:

1. **Content Marketing**: Create valuable content that attracts and engages your target audience. This could be blog posts, free tutorials, or social media content related to your product. Content marketing helps build trust and authority, driving traffic to your product pages.

2. **Email Marketing**: Build an email list to communicate directly with your audience. Use lead magnets (free content offered in exchange for email addresses) to grow your list. Send regular updates about new products, promotions, and valuable content to keep your audience engaged.

3. **Social Media Marketing**: Utilize platforms like Instagram, Facebook, Twitter, and Pinterest to showcase your products. Share engaging content, use relevant hashtags, and interact with your audience. Paid advertising on these platforms can also be highly effective.

4. **Search Engine Optimization (SEO)**: Optimize your product pages and content for search engines. Use relevant keywords, meta descriptions, and quality content to improve your search rankings. Higher visibility on search engines leads to more organic traffic.

5. **Partnerships and Affiliates**: Collaborate with bloggers, influencers, and other creators who can promote your products to their audiences. Affiliate programs can incentivize others to sell your products in exchange for a commission.

Setting Up a Sales Funnel

A sales funnel guides potential customers from initial awareness of your product to making a purchase. Here's how to set up an effective sales funnel:

1. **Awareness**: Attract potential customers with content marketing, social media, and paid advertising. Create engaging content that addresses their needs and interests.

2. **Interest**: Capture leads by offering valuable content in exchange for their contact information. This could be a free ebook, a webinar, or a sample of your course.

3. **Consideration**: Nurture your leads with email marketing. Send them useful information, case studies, and testimonials to build trust and demonstrate the value of your product.

4. **Decision**: Provide clear calls to action and make the purchasing process as smooth as possible. Offer incentives like discounts or bonuses to encourage conversions.

5. **Action**: Once a customer makes a purchase, ensure a seamless delivery of the product. Follow up with thank-you emails, and offer additional support or resources.

Showcasing Your Own Offers: PassionFuze

In my journey of digital product creation, I've developed several resources to help others succeed. One of the most comprehensive offerings is PassionFuze, a platform that teaches you how to create, launch, and sell digital products effectively. Here's what you can expect from PassionFuze:

1. **Comprehensive Training**: PassionFuze offers in-depth training on every aspect of digital product creation, from idea generation and content creation to marketing and sales. It's designed for both beginners and experienced creators looking to refine their skills.

2. **Practical Resources**: You'll get access to templates, checklists, and tools that streamline the creation process. These resources save you time and ensure you don't miss any critical steps.

3. **Community Support**: Join a community of like-minded creators who share their experiences, offer support, and provide valuable feedback. Networking with others can lead to collaborations and new opportunities.

4. **Expert Guidance**: Learn from industry experts who have successfully created and sold digital products. Their insights

and tips can help you avoid common pitfalls and achieve your goals faster.

5. **Continuous Updates**: The digital landscape is constantly evolving. PassionFuze provides regular updates to keep you informed about the latest trends, tools, and strategies.

Leveraging Platforms Like WarriorPlus and JVZoo

In addition to mainstream platforms like Gumroad and Teachable, consider using specialized platforms like WarriorPlus and JVZoo to reach a broader audience. These platforms are particularly effective for digital marketers and product creators. Here's how to leverage them:

1. **WarriorPlus**: Known for its active community of digital marketers, WarriorPlus offers tools for product creation, sales, and affiliate management. Create a compelling product page, set up an affiliate program, and leverage the platform's community to drive sales.

2. **JVZoo**: Similar to WarriorPlus, JVZoo focuses on digital products and affiliate marketing. It provides robust tools for creating and launching products, managing affiliates, and tracking sales. Utilize JVZoo's network to expand your reach and boost sales.

3. **Affiliate Programs**: Both platforms allow you to set up affiliate programs, enabling others to promote your products in exchange for a commission. This can significantly increase your sales and expand your audience.

Real-Life Examples and Case Studies

Learning from real-life examples can provide valuable insights and inspiration. Here are some case studies of successful digital product creators:

1. **Ebook Success**: Jane, a fitness enthusiast, created an ebook on home workouts. She validated her idea through market research and created engaging content with high-quality images. Using Gumroad, she marketed her ebook through her

blog and social media, leveraging content marketing and email campaigns. Within six months, Jane generated over $10,000 in sales.

2. **Online Course Triumph**: Mark, a software developer, decided to create an online course on Python programming. He outlined his course, recorded high-quality video lessons, and used Teachable for distribution. By offering a free introductory webinar, he attracted a large audience. Through email marketing and SEO, Mark's course enrollment grew steadily, earning him a monthly income of $5,000.

3. **Graphic Design Templates**: Sarah, a graphic designer, created a series of PowerPoint templates and social media graphics. She used Canva for design and listed her products on Etsy and Creative Market. By optimizing her listings with relevant keywords and promoting her designs on Pinterest, Sarah built a loyal customer base. Her consistent sales resulted in a monthly income of $3,000.

Scaling Your Digital Product Business

As your digital product business grows, consider these strategies to scale effectively:

1. **Expanding Product Lines**: Introduce new products regularly to keep your offerings fresh and engaging. This could include new ebooks, additional courses, or updated software versions.

2. **Exploring New Markets**: Expand your reach to new geographical markets. Offer your products in different languages or tailor them to specific regional needs.

3. **Increasing Advertising Spend**: Invest more in advertising channels that have proven effective. This can amplify your reach and drive more sales.

4. **Building a Team**: As your business grows, consider hiring freelancers or full-time staff to help with content creation, marketing, and customer support. This allows you to focus on strategic planning and business development.

5. **Leveraging Automation**: Use automation tools to streamline repetitive tasks like email marketing, social media posting, and customer support. This saves time and allows you to focus on high-value activities.

Overcoming Challenges in Digital Product Creation

Creating and selling digital products comes with its own set of challenges. Here's how to overcome some common obstacles:

1. **Technical Issues**: If you're not tech-savvy, creating digital products can be daunting. Invest time in learning the necessary tools or hire professionals to help with technical aspects like website development, video editing, or software coding.

2. **Marketing Struggles**: Effective marketing is crucial for success. If you're struggling, consider taking online courses in digital marketing or hiring a marketing expert. Focus on understanding your audience and tailoring your marketing efforts to their needs.

3. **Content Creation Burnout**: Creating high-quality content can be exhausting. Break the process into manageable chunks, set realistic deadlines, and take regular breaks to avoid burnout. Collaborate with others to share the workload.

4. **Competition**: The digital marketplace is competitive. Differentiate your products by offering unique value, high quality, and exceptional customer service. Continuously improve your offerings based on customer feedback and market trends.

5. **Legal and Financial Concerns**: Ensure you're compliant with legal requirements like copyrights, trademarks, and data protection regulations. Consult with legal and financial advisors to protect your business and manage your finances effectively.

Future Trends in Digital Product Creation

Staying ahead of future trends can give you a competitive edge. Here are some trends to watch in the digital product space:

1. **Micro-Learning**: Bite-sized educational content is becoming increasingly popular. Consider creating short, focused courses or mini-guides that cater to busy learners.

2. **Interactive Content**: Interactive elements like quizzes, polls, and gamified experiences can enhance engagement. Incorporate these into your digital products to create a more immersive experience.

3. **Personalization**: Personalized content tailored to individual preferences and needs can significantly enhance user experience. Use data and analytics to customize your offerings.

4. **Augmented and Virtual Reality**: AR and VR technologies are transforming digital learning and entertainment. Explore how these technologies can be integrated into your products to offer unique experiences.

5. **Subscription Models**: Subscription-based services provide a steady revenue stream and build long-term customer relationships. Consider offering subscription options for continuous access to your content.

Creating and selling digital products is a powerful way to build a sustainable and lucrative business.

By leveraging the right tools, effective marketing strategies, and continuous innovation, you can achieve significant success in the digital marketplace.

With dedication, strategic planning, and a proactive approach, achieving a monthly income of $1,000 or more from digital product creation is well within your reach. Remember, the key to success lies in providing value to your audience, continuously improving your offerings, and staying adaptable to market trends.

Let's embark on this exciting journey together and unlock the limitless potential of digital product creation in 2024 and beyond.

Chapter 3: E-commerce and Dropshipping

Welcome to the dynamic world of e-commerce, where the digital marketplace provides endless opportunities to build a profitable business. In 2024, e-commerce, especially through the dropshipping model, stands out as a viable and lucrative option for generating substantial income with low upfront investment. Let's explore how you can leverage this business model to achieve and surpass your financial goals.

Understanding E-commerce and Dropshipping

E-commerce involves buying and selling goods and services online. Dropshipping, a specific e-commerce model, allows you to sell products without holding any inventory. Instead, when a customer makes a purchase from your online store, the order is sent to a third-party supplier who ships the product directly to the customer. This model minimizes risk and capital requirements, making it an attractive option for new entrepreneurs.

Setting Up Your E-commerce Store

Creating a successful e-commerce store involves several key steps:

1. **Choosing a Niche**: Selecting a market niche that you are passionate about and that has good demand is crucial. A well-defined niche helps you target your marketing efforts more effectively and build a loyal customer base. Research trends, identify gaps in the market, and focus on a niche where you can offer unique value.

2. **Selecting a Platform**: Platforms like Shopify, WooCommerce (for WordPress users), and BigCommerce provide robust tools to create an online store. These platforms offer various templates, integration options, and customer support to facilitate your business operations. I personally recommend Shopify for its ease of use and extensive app ecosystem.

3. **Setting Up Your Store**: Customize your store's design to reflect your brand. Ensure that the website is user-friendly, with clear navigation and a professional appearance to encourage purchases. Pay attention to the details – high-quality images, compelling product descriptions, and a seamless checkout process can significantly impact your conversion rates.

Finding Reliable Suppliers

A reliable supplier is crucial in the dropshipping model. Your supplier's ability to provide high-quality products and reliable shipping directly impacts your reputation. Consider these points when choosing suppliers:

1. **Quality and Reliability**: Order samples to check the quality of the products. Assess the supplier's shipping times and packaging to ensure they meet your standards. Remember, your reputation hinges on the quality of the products you sell.

2. **Communication**: Establish clear communication channels. Your supplier should be responsive and able to handle inquiries and issues promptly. Good communication can prevent misunderstandings and ensure smooth operations.

3. **Scalability**: Ensure the supplier can scale with your growing business. They should be able to handle increases in order volume without compromising quality or efficiency. This is particularly important during peak seasons like holidays.

4. **Platforms for Finding Suppliers**: Platforms like AliExpress and Oberlo connect you with numerous suppliers worldwide. These platforms also integrate easily with major e-commerce platforms like Shopify, simplifying the process of adding products to your store.

Marketing Your Products

Effective marketing is vital in driving traffic to your e-commerce store and converting visitors into customers. Here are some key marketing strategies:

1. **Social Media Marketing**: Use platforms like Instagram, Facebook, and Pinterest to promote your products. These platforms allow for rich visual content that can showcase your products attractively, enhancing engagement and conversion rates. Post regularly, engage with your audience, and use paid advertising to reach a larger audience.

2. **Content Marketing**: Develop valuable content related to your niche. Blog posts, tutorials, and videos can attract and engage your target audience, build your brand's authority, and improve SEO. For example, if you're selling fitness products, create content about workout routines, nutrition tips, and product reviews.

3. **Email Marketing**: Build an email list from the onset. Offer incentives like discounts or exclusive content in exchange for email sign-ups. Use this channel to keep your audience informed about new products, sales, or content. Email marketing can be highly personalized, making it an effective tool for driving sales.

4. **Paid Advertising**: Invest in PPC (pay-per-click) advertising on Google, Facebook, or Instagram to drive targeted traffic to your site. Adjust and optimize your ad campaigns based on performance metrics and ROI. Use retargeting ads to reach visitors who have previously interacted with your site but haven't made a purchase.

5. **SEO**: Optimize your website for search engines to improve visibility. Include relevant keywords, meta descriptions, and quality content to rank higher in search results. SEO is a long-term strategy but can drive consistent organic traffic to your store.

Providing Excellent Customer Service

Outstanding customer service can set your e-commerce store apart from competitors. Respond promptly to customer inquiries, resolve issues efficiently, and exceed customer expectations to foster loyalty and encourage repeat business. Here are some tips:

1. **Clear Communication**: Provide clear and timely communication at every stage of the purchase process. Use automated emails to update customers on their order status and provide tracking information.

2. **Easy Returns and Refunds**: Make your return and refund policies clear and easy to find. A hassle-free return process builds trust and increases customer satisfaction.

3. **Personal Touch**: Personalize your interactions with customers. Address them by name, thank them for their purchase, and follow up to ensure they're satisfied with their order.

4. **Customer Feedback**: Encourage and act on customer feedback. Use reviews and testimonials to improve your products and services. Positive reviews can also enhance your credibility and attract new customers.

Monitoring and Analyzing Your Store's Performance

Using analytics tools to track your store's performance is essential for making informed decisions and optimizing your business strategy. Here's how to effectively monitor and analyze your e-commerce store:

1. **Google Analytics**: Set up Google Analytics to track website traffic, user behavior, and conversion rates. Analyze this data to understand where your traffic is coming from, which products are popular, and how visitors are interacting with your site.

2. **Sales Metrics**: Monitor key sales metrics such as average order value, customer acquisition cost, and lifetime value. These metrics provide insights into your store's profitability and growth potential.

3. **Customer Insights**: Use tools like Shopify's built-in analytics or third-party apps to gather customer insights. Understand your customers' demographics, preferences, and purchasing behavior to tailor your marketing efforts.

4. **A/B Testing**: Conduct A/B testing to compare different versions of your website, product pages, or marketing

campaigns. This helps you determine what works best and make data-driven improvements.

Scaling Your E-commerce Business

As your e-commerce business grows, consider these strategies to scale effectively:

1. **Expand Product Lines**: Introduce new products regularly to keep your offerings fresh and attract repeat customers. Conduct market research to identify trending products and add them to your inventory.

2. **Explore New Markets**: Consider expanding your reach to international markets. Ensure your e-commerce platform supports multiple currencies and shipping options. Localize your website content and marketing campaigns to resonate with different regions.

3. **Increase Advertising Spend**: Invest more in advertising channels that have proven effective for your business. Use data from your analytics tools to allocate your budget to the highest-performing campaigns.

4. **Automate Processes**: Use automation tools to streamline repetitive tasks like inventory management, order processing, and customer communication. This frees up your time to focus on strategic growth initiatives.

5. **Build a Team**: As your business grows, consider hiring additional staff or freelancers to handle customer service, marketing, and operations. Building a team allows you to scale your business without being overwhelmed by day-to-day tasks.

Overcoming Challenges in E-commerce and Dropshipping

Running an e-commerce business comes with its own set of challenges. Here's how to overcome some common obstacles:

1. **Finding Reliable Suppliers**: Not all suppliers are reliable. To mitigate this risk, work with multiple suppliers and maintain good relationships with them. Regularly review their performance and be prepared to switch suppliers if necessary.

2. **Managing Inventory**: Even in a dropshipping model, managing inventory can be challenging. Use inventory management software to keep track of stock levels, forecast demand, and avoid stockouts.

3. **Handling Returns**: Returns are inevitable in e-commerce. Have a clear return policy and streamline your return process to handle returns efficiently. Work closely with your suppliers to manage returns and ensure customer satisfaction.

4. **Shipping Delays**: Shipping delays can negatively impact customer satisfaction. Set realistic delivery expectations, provide accurate tracking information, and communicate proactively with customers about any delays.

5. **Dealing with Competition**: The e-commerce space is highly competitive. Differentiate your store by offering unique products, exceptional customer service, and a compelling brand story. Focus on building a loyal customer base rather than competing solely on price.

Case Studies of Successful E-commerce and Dropshipping Businesses

Learning from real-life examples can provide valuable insights and inspiration. Here are some case studies of successful e-commerce and dropshipping businesses:

1. **Fashion Dropshipping**: Emma started a fashion dropshipping store focusing on eco-friendly clothing. She sourced products from reliable suppliers who shared her commitment to sustainability. Through effective social media marketing and collaborations with eco-conscious influencers, Emma's store quickly gained traction. By offering unique, high-quality products and exceptional customer service, she achieved a monthly income of $10,000 within a year.

2. **Home Decor E-commerce**: John launched an online store selling handmade home decor items. He partnered with local artisans and used Shopify to set up his store. John's content marketing strategy included blog posts about interior design trends and DIY home decor tips, which drove organic traffic to his site. By leveraging email marketing and SEO, John built a loyal customer base and generated a steady monthly income of $5,000.

3. **Fitness Products Dropshipping**: Lisa created a dropshipping store specializing in fitness products, such as resistance bands and yoga mats. She used Oberlo to source products and integrated her store with Shopify. Lisa's marketing strategy included creating workout videos and tutorials on YouTube, driving traffic to her store. Her focus on high-quality content and customer engagement helped her reach a monthly income of $7,500.

Future Trends in E-commerce and Dropshipping

Staying ahead of future trends can give you a competitive edge in the e-commerce space. Here are some trends to watch in 2024:

1. **Personalization**: Personalized shopping experiences are becoming increasingly important. Use data and AI to offer personalized product recommendations, tailored marketing messages, and customized shopping experiences.

2. **Sustainability**: Consumers are increasingly conscious of sustainability. Consider sourcing eco-friendly products, using sustainable packaging, and highlighting your commitment to sustainability in your marketing efforts.

3. **Mobile Commerce**: Mobile commerce is growing rapidly. Ensure your e-commerce store is mobile-friendly, with a responsive design and a seamless mobile shopping experience.

4. **Voice Search**: With the rise of smart speakers and voice assistants, optimizing your store for voice search can enhance visibility and attract more customers. Focus on long-tail

keywords and natural language in your product descriptions and SEO strategy.

5. **Augmented Reality (AR)**: AR technology is transforming the shopping experience by allowing customers to visualize products in their own space. Consider integrating AR features into your e-commerce store to enhance the customer experience and drive sales.

E-commerce and dropshipping offer substantial opportunities to build a profitable business with low upfront investment. This is what helped me get started back in 2012, up until 2014. I stopped with dropshipping because I found my new passion, into affiliate marketing more exciting and faceless.

By choosing a profitable niche, partnering with reliable suppliers, and implementing robust marketing strategies, you can achieve and exceed your financial goals.

Focus on providing excellent customer service, leveraging analytics to optimize performance, and staying ahead of industry trends to ensure long-term success.

Chapter 4: Dividend Investing

Welcome to the strategic world of dividend investing, where your money works for you by generating a steady stream of passive income. In 2024, dividend investing remains a powerful strategy for achieving financial independence. By carefully selecting stocks that pay regular dividends and managing your portfolio wisely, you can build a reliable income stream. Let's dive into the key factors, strategies, and tools that will help you consistently achieve a monthly income of $1,000 or more from dividends.

Understanding Dividend Investing

Dividend investing involves purchasing stocks that pay dividends, which are portions of a company's earnings distributed to shareholders at regular intervals. This investment strategy not only provides regular income but also offers the potential for capital appreciation. Unlike fixed-income securities, dividends from stocks can increase over time, offering an inflation-beating growth component.

Benefits of Dividend Investing

1. **Income Generation**: Dividends provide a source of regular, predictable income, which can be especially appealing for those seeking financial stability or supplemental income.

2. **Reinvestment Opportunities**: Dividends can be reinvested to purchase additional shares, compounding your investment and potentially increasing future income.

3. **Risk Mitigation**: Typically, companies that regularly pay dividends are well-established and financially stable, reducing investment risk compared to non-dividend-paying stocks.

Key Factors to Consider in Dividend Investing

Selecting the right dividend stocks is crucial for successful investing. Here are the key factors to consider:

1. **Dividend Yield**: This is the percentage ratio of a company's annual dividend compared to its stock price. While a high dividend yield is attractive, it's essential to assess the sustainability of dividends. Extremely high yields may not be sustainable in the long term.

2. **Dividend Growth**: Look for companies with a history of increasing their dividends. Steady dividend growth often indicates robust financial health and a commitment to returning value to shareholders.

3. **Payout Ratio**: The payout ratio (the proportion of earnings paid out as dividends) is a crucial indicator of dividend sustainability. A ratio that is too high (generally above 80%) may signal that the company is not reinvesting enough in its own growth, which could jeopardize future dividends.

4. **Company Fundamentals**: Analyze the company's overall financial health, including revenue growth, earnings stability, cash flow, and debt levels. Companies with strong fundamentals are more likely to maintain and grow dividends.

Diversifying Your Portfolio

Diversification is a cornerstone of risk management in dividend investing. By spreading your investments across various sectors and industries, you can reduce the impact of any single investment's poor performance on your overall portfolio. Here's how to diversify effectively:

1. **Sector Diversification**: Invest in dividend-paying stocks from different sectors such as technology, healthcare, consumer goods, utilities, and financials. Each sector has its own economic cycles and risks, so diversification can protect your portfolio from sector-specific downturns.

2. **Geographical Diversification**: Consider investing in international dividend stocks to gain exposure to global markets. This not only diversifies your portfolio but also provides opportunities to benefit from different economic conditions and growth prospects.

3. **Dividend Reinvestment Plans (DRIPs)**: Many companies offer DRIPs, which automatically reinvest dividends into additional shares, often at a discount and without brokerage fees. DRIPs are an excellent way to increase the compound growth of your investments, as they allow dividends to generate more dividends.

Using Bybit for Trading and Diversification

In addition to traditional dividend investing, incorporating cryptocurrency investments can add another layer of diversification to your portfolio. Bybit, one of my favorite exchanges, offers a reliable platform for trading cryptocurrencies. You can sign up for Bybit using my referral link: Bybit Sign-Up.

Bybit provides various trading options, including spot trading and derivatives, allowing you to diversify your investments beyond traditional stocks. While cryptocurrencies can be more volatile, they also offer the potential for significant returns. Combining traditional dividend stocks with cryptocurrency investments can enhance your portfolio's overall growth potential.

Strategies for Successful Dividend Investing

Implementing the right strategies can maximize your returns and minimize risks. Here are some effective strategies for successful dividend investing:

1. **Blue-Chip Stocks**: Focus on established, blue-chip companies with a strong history of dividend payments. These companies typically have stable earnings, strong balance sheets, and a commitment to returning value to shareholders.

2. **Dividend Aristocrats**: Consider investing in Dividend Aristocrats, which are companies that have consistently increased their dividends for at least 25 consecutive years. These companies are often leaders in their industries and have demonstrated financial resilience.

3. **High-Yield Dividend Stocks**: While high-yield stocks can provide substantial income, be cautious and ensure the dividends are sustainable. Look for companies with a moderate payout ratio and strong cash flow to support their dividend payments.

4. **Dividend ETFs**: Exchange-Traded Funds (ETFs) that focus on dividend-paying stocks can provide instant diversification. Dividend ETFs often include a basket of high-quality dividend stocks, reducing the risk associated with individual stock investments.

5. **Reinvesting Dividends**: Use DRIPs to automatically reinvest dividends and benefit from compounding growth. This strategy allows your investments to grow exponentially over time.

Portfolio Management

Managing your dividend investment portfolio involves several strategies to maximize returns and minimize risks. Here's how to effectively manage your portfolio:

1. **Regular Monitoring**: Regularly review your stock positions and the financial health of the companies you invest in. Be alert to changes in business performance or economic conditions that might affect dividend payments.

2. **Rebalancing**: Periodically rebalance your portfolio to maintain your desired asset allocation. This involves selling overperforming assets and buying underperforming ones to ensure your portfolio remains diversified.

3. **Tax Considerations**: Understand the tax implications of dividend income, as it can impact your net returns. Dividend income is taxable, and the rate can vary based on your overall income and tax laws. Consult with a tax advisor to optimize your tax strategy.

4. **Long-Term Perspective**: Dividend investing is typically a long-term strategy. Focus on the long-term growth potential of your investments rather than short-term market fluctuations. Patience and discipline are key to successful dividend investing.

Real-Life Examples of Successful Dividend Investing

Learning from real-life examples can provide valuable insights and inspiration. Here are some case studies of successful dividend investors:

1. **Utilities**: Utility companies are typically stable and reliable dividend payers because of their regulated nature and consistent demand. For example, Duke Energy has a long history of paying dividends and offers a steady income stream for investors.

2. **Consumer Staples**: Companies in the consumer staples sector often perform well even during economic downturns, as demand for essential products remains stable. Procter & Gamble, known for its diverse portfolio of consumer products, has consistently increased its dividends, making it a popular choice for dividend investors.

3. **Real Estate Investment Trusts (REITs)**: REITs are required by law to distribute at least 90% of their taxable income to shareholders, making them high-yield investments. Realty Income Corporation, known as "The Monthly Dividend Company," is a prime example of a REIT that provides reliable monthly dividends.

Managing Risks in Dividend Investing

While dividend investing offers numerous benefits, it's essential to manage risks effectively. Here are some strategies to mitigate risks:

1. **Economic Cycles**: Be aware of how economic cycles can impact different sectors. For example, interest rate changes can significantly affect utilities and REITs. Diversify your portfolio to include stocks from various sectors to balance out sector-specific risks.

2. **Company-Specific Risks**: Monitor the financial health of the companies you invest in. Look for red flags such as declining revenues, increasing debt levels, or changes in management. Regularly review earnings reports and stay updated on company news.

3. **Market Volatility**: While dividend stocks tend to be less volatile than growth stocks, they are not immune to market fluctuations. Maintain a long-term perspective and avoid making impulsive decisions based on short-term market movements.

4. **Regulatory Changes**: Stay informed about potential regulatory changes that could affect your investments. For example, changes in tax laws or industry regulations can impact a company's profitability and ability to pay dividends.

Tools and Resources for Dividend Investors

Utilizing the right tools and resources can enhance your dividend investing strategy. Here are some valuable tools to consider:

1. **Stock Screeners**: Use stock screeners to filter dividend stocks based on specific criteria such as yield, payout ratio, and dividend growth history. Websites like Finviz and Dividend.com offer robust screening tools.

2. **Investment Newsletters**: Subscribe to investment newsletters that focus on dividend investing. These newsletters provide insights, stock recommendations, and market analysis to help you make informed decisions.

3. **Financial News Websites**: Stay updated with the latest financial news and analysis. Websites like Bloomberg, CNBC, and Seeking Alpha offer comprehensive coverage of market trends and company performance.

4. **Investment Apps**: Use investment apps like Robinhood, M1 Finance, and E*TRADE to manage your portfolio on the go. These apps offer features such as real-time market data, portfolio tracking, and dividend reinvestment options.

Building a Dividend Investing Plan

Creating a well-defined dividend investing plan is essential for achieving your financial goals. Here's how to build a comprehensive plan:

1. **Set Clear Objectives**: Define your financial goals and objectives. Determine how much monthly income you want to generate from dividends and the timeframe to achieve it.

2. **Assess Your Risk Tolerance**: Understand your risk tolerance and investment preferences. This will guide your asset allocation and stock selection.

3. **Create a Diversified Portfolio**: Build a diversified portfolio of dividend-paying stocks across various sectors and geographical regions. Use ETFs and mutual funds to achieve instant diversification.

4. **Implement a Reinvestment Strategy**: Decide whether you will reinvest your dividends or take them as cash. Reinvesting dividends can accelerate the growth of your portfolio.

5. **Monitor and Adjust**: Regularly review your portfolio's performance and make adjustments as needed. Stay informed about market trends and economic conditions that may impact your investments.

Achieving $1,000 Monthly Income from Dividends

Achieving a monthly income of $1,000 from dividends requires careful planning, strategic investing, and disciplined management. Here's a step-by-step approach to reach this goal:

1. **Calculate the Required Investment**: Determine the amount of capital needed to generate $1,000 in monthly dividends. For example, if your average dividend yield is 4%, you would need an investment of $300,000 to achieve this income ($300,000 * 4% / 12 = $1,000).

2. **Identify High-Quality Dividend Stocks**: Focus on high-quality dividend stocks with sustainable payouts and strong growth potential. Use the key factors discussed earlier to select the best stocks for your portfolio.

3. **Invest Regularly**: Make regular contributions to your investment portfolio. Use dollar-cost averaging to spread your investments over time, reducing the impact of market volatility.

4. **Reinvest Dividends**: Utilize DRIPs to reinvest your dividends and benefit from compounding growth. This strategy

accelerates the growth of your portfolio and increases your dividend income over time.

5. **Monitor and Optimize**: Regularly review your portfolio and make necessary adjustments. Optimize your investments by reallocating funds to higher-performing stocks or sectors.

Dividend investing is a powerful strategy for generating passive income and achieving financial independence.

By carefully selecting high-quality dividend stocks, diversifying your portfolio, and reinvesting your dividends, you can build a reliable income stream. Incorporating cryptocurrency investments through platforms like Bybit can further enhance your portfolio's growth potential.

Chapter 5: Real Estate Crowdfunding

Welcome to the revolutionary world of real estate crowdfunding, where property investment is no longer reserved for the wealthy elite. Real estate crowdfunding democratizes property investment, allowing you to pool resources with other investors to fund real estate projects. This innovative approach opens the door to residential, commercial, and large-scale properties with minimal upfront capital. Let's explore how you can leverage real estate crowdfunding to achieve significant returns and a stable monthly income.

Understanding Real Estate Crowdfunding

Real estate crowdfunding allows multiple investors to pool their financial resources to invest in real estate projects. These projects can range from residential properties and commercial developments to large-scale real estate portfolios. Platforms that offer these opportunities act as a bridge between investors and developers or property owners needing capital.

Advantages of Real Estate Crowdfunding

1. **Accessibility**: You can start investing with a relatively small amount of money compared to traditional real estate investments, making it accessible to a wider audience.

2. **Diversification**: This method offers an excellent opportunity to diversify your investment portfolio beyond stocks and bonds into real estate, which often moves counter to the trends of traditional financial markets.

3. **Potential Returns**: Real estate crowdfunding can offer attractive returns through rental income as well as property value appreciation.

4. **Passive Income**: Most investments in real estate crowdfunding are passive, meaning you do not have to manage the property yourself, which is typically handled by experienced property managers.

How to Get Started with Real Estate Crowdfunding

Starting with real estate crowdfunding involves several steps to ensure you make informed and strategic investment decisions.

1. **Choosing the Right Platform**: Research and select a crowdfunding platform that aligns with your investment goals. Some platforms might focus on residential properties, while others might offer commercial real estate investments. Examples include Fundrise, RealtyMogul, and CrowdStreet.

2. **Due Diligence**: Before investing, conduct thorough due diligence on the property and the deal. Understand the market analysis, project plan, and financial projections. Also, review the track record of the person or company offering the investment.

3. **Understanding the Terms**: Be clear about the investment's terms, including your rights as an investor, the timeframe, expected returns, fee structure, and the exit strategy.

4. **Start Small**: If you are new to real estate investments, start with a small amount to understand the process and risks involved. As you gain experience and confidence, you can gradually increase your investment.

Key Strategies for Successful Real Estate Crowdfunding

Implementing the right strategies can maximize your returns and minimize risks. Here are some key strategies for successful real estate crowdfunding:

1. **Diversification Within Real Estate**: Just as diversifying across different asset classes is essential, diversifying within your real estate investments can help mitigate risks. Invest in different types of properties (e.g., residential, commercial, industrial) and in different geographical locations.

2. **Active Portfolio Management**: Regularly review your investments' performance and the health of the real estate market. Be prepared to adjust your portfolio as needed based on performance and evolving market conditions.

3. **Leverage Expert Advice**: Utilize the expertise available through the crowdfunding platform, and consider consulting with real estate professionals to enhance your understanding and strategies.

Real Estate Crowdfunding Platforms

Choosing the right platform is crucial for your success in real estate crowdfunding. Here are some leading platforms that provide robust opportunities for investors:

1. **Fundrise**: Fundrise offers a variety of investment options, including eREITs and eFunds, which allow you to invest in diversified portfolios of real estate assets. Fundrise is known for its user-friendly interface and low minimum investment requirements, making it accessible to new investors.

2. **RealtyMogul**: RealtyMogul provides opportunities to invest in both individual properties and REITs (Real Estate Investment

Trusts). The platform offers a wide range of commercial real estate projects, from office buildings to multi-family apartments.

3. **CrowdStreet**: CrowdStreet focuses on high-quality commercial real estate investments. It connects accredited investors with real estate developers and offers detailed information on each project, including financial projections and market analysis.

4. **DiversyFund**: DiversyFund operates its own REIT, allowing you to invest in a diversified portfolio of real estate assets. The platform focuses on multi-family properties and aims to provide steady cash flow and long-term appreciation.

Conducting Thorough Due Diligence

Thorough due diligence is critical to making informed investment decisions in real estate crowdfunding. Here's how to conduct due diligence effectively:

1. **Market Analysis**: Understand the local real estate market where the property is located. Look at factors like population growth, employment rates, and economic trends. A strong local market increases the likelihood of property appreciation and rental income stability.

2. **Property Evaluation**: Evaluate the property itself, including its location, condition, and potential for income generation. Review any available inspection reports and assessments. Properties in prime locations or areas with high demand are more likely to perform well.

3. **Developer Track Record**: Investigate the track record of the developer or sponsor managing the project. Look at their history of completed projects, their success rate, and any feedback from previous investors. A reputable developer with a proven track record reduces the risk of project failure.

4. **Financial Projections**: Scrutinize the financial projections provided by the crowdfunding platform. Understand the

assumptions behind these projections and consider various scenarios, including worst-case outcomes. Verify the projected returns, expenses, and timeline.

5. **Legal Considerations**: Review the legal documents associated with the investment, including the offering memorandum, subscription agreement, and operating agreement. Ensure you understand your rights and obligations as an investor, as well as the terms and conditions of the investment.

Managing Your Real Estate Crowdfunding Portfolio

Effective portfolio management is essential for maximizing returns and minimizing risks. Here are some tips for managing your real estate crowdfunding portfolio:

1. **Regular Monitoring**: Keep track of your investments and the performance of the properties you've invested in. Use the reporting tools provided by the crowdfunding platform to monitor rental income, property value, and overall project progress.

2. **Reinvestment Strategy**: Reinvest your earnings to compound your returns. Whether it's rental income or proceeds from property sales, reinvesting can accelerate the growth of your portfolio.

3. **Stay Informed**: Stay updated on market trends and economic factors that could impact your real estate investments. Subscribe to real estate newsletters, follow industry news, and participate in webinars or events hosted by crowdfunding platforms.

4. **Risk Management**: Diversify your investments to spread risk. Avoid over-concentrating your portfolio in a single property type, location, or developer. Consider setting aside a portion of your portfolio in more conservative investments to balance higher-risk projects.

5. **Exit Strategy**: Have a clear exit strategy for each investment. Understand the timeline and conditions under which you can

sell your investment or withdraw funds. Be prepared to adjust your strategy based on market conditions and project performance.

Real-Life Examples of Successful Real Estate Crowdfunding

Learning from real-life examples can provide valuable insights and inspiration. Here are some case studies of successful real estate crowdfunding investments:

1. **Residential Apartment Complex**: Sarah invested in a residential apartment complex through Fundrise. The project was located in a growing metropolitan area with high demand for rental properties. Over three years, the property's value appreciated significantly, and Sarah received steady rental income, resulting in an annual return of 10%.

2. **Commercial Office Building**: Mark invested in a commercial office building in a major city through RealtyMogul. The building was fully leased to high-credit tenants, providing stable rental income. After five years, the property was sold at a profit, and Mark's total return on investment was 12% per year.

3. **Mixed-Use Development**: Lisa invested in a mixed-use development project through CrowdStreet. The project included retail, office, and residential units in a rapidly developing area. The diverse income streams and the area's growth potential resulted in a 15% annual return over four years.

Overcoming Challenges in Real Estate Crowdfunding

While real estate crowdfunding offers numerous benefits, it also comes with challenges. Here's how to overcome some common obstacles:

1. **Market Fluctuations**: Real estate markets can be volatile. To mitigate this risk, diversify your investments across different property types and geographical locations. Stay informed about market trends and economic conditions that could impact your investments.

2. **Liquidity Risk**: Real estate investments are generally less liquid than stocks or bonds. Understand the investment's timeline and be prepared for the possibility of holding your investment longer than initially planned. Choose investments with clear exit strategies and flexible terms if liquidity is a concern.

3. **Platform Reliability**: The success of your investment can partly depend on the crowdfunding platform's stability and management quality. Research the platform's reputation, track record, and financial health before committing your funds.

4. **Regulatory Changes**: Be aware of potential regulatory changes that could affect real estate investments in your region or nationally. Stay updated on real estate laws, tax policies, and other regulations that could impact your returns.

5. **Project Delays**: Construction and development projects can face delays due to various factors such as permitting issues, labor shortages, or supply chain disruptions. Evaluate the developer's contingency plans and ability to manage delays effectively.

Future Trends in Real Estate Crowdfunding

Staying ahead of future trends can give you a competitive edge in real estate crowdfunding. Here are some trends to watch in 2024:

1. **Technology Integration**: Advances in technology, such as blockchain and artificial intelligence, are transforming real estate crowdfunding. Blockchain can enhance transparency and security in transactions, while AI can improve market analysis and investment decision-making.

2. **Sustainable Investments**: There is a growing emphasis on sustainability in real estate. Investing in eco-friendly and

energy-efficient properties can attract socially conscious investors and tenants, potentially enhancing property values and returns.

3. **Urban Redevelopment**: Urban redevelopment projects are gaining traction as cities seek to revitalize older neighborhoods. These projects can offer significant returns but also come with higher risks. Evaluate the potential impact of urban renewal on property values and demand.

4. **Fractional Ownership**: Fractional ownership is becoming more popular, allowing investors to buy a fraction of a property rather than the entire asset. This approach lowers the barrier to entry and enables greater diversification within real estate portfolios.

5. **Global Investment Opportunities**: Real estate crowdfunding platforms are expanding their reach, offering investment opportunities in international markets. Diversifying globally can provide exposure to different economic cycles and growth prospects.

Real estate crowdfunding presents a unique opportunity to engage in property investment without the need for significant upfront capital.

Chapter 6: Affiliate Marketing

Welcome to the exciting world of affiliate marketing, a powerful strategy that can generate substantial income by promoting products or services through unique affiliate links.

Affiliate marketing has been a cornerstone of my business, enabling me to earn commissions that sometimes exceed $1,000 a day and average between $5,000 and $10,000 a month. Let's explore how you can achieve similar success by leveraging the right platforms and strategies.

Understanding Affiliate Marketing

Affiliate marketing is a performance-based marketing model where businesses pay external publishers (affiliates) to generate traffic or leads to the company's products and services. Affiliates earn a commission when the traffic they generate results in a sale. This model benefits both the affiliate and the company by extending the company's reach and offering affiliates an opportunity to earn based on their performance.

Key Components of Affiliate Marketing

1. **Affiliate Links**: Unique URLs provided by the affiliate program that track the traffic and sales generated by the affiliate.
2. **Commissions**: The earnings an affiliate receives for each sale, lead, or action generated through their affiliate links.
3. **Cookies**: Small files stored on a user's device that track their activity. Affiliate cookies typically have a duration, ensuring affiliates get credit for sales made within a specific timeframe.

Choosing the Right Niche

Success in affiliate marketing begins with choosing a niche that is both interesting to you and profitable. Here's how to choose the right niche:

1. **Passion and Expertise**: Select a niche that aligns with your interests and expertise. When you are passionate about a subject, creating content becomes more enjoyable and authentic.
2. **Market Demand**: Research market demand for your chosen niche. Use tools like Google Trends, keyword research tools, and market analysis reports to gauge interest and competition.
3. **Profitability**: Consider the profitability of the niche. Look for niches with high-ticket items or recurring revenue opportunities, such as subscriptions or membership sites.

Selecting the Right Affiliate Programs

Not all affiliate programs are created equal. Look for programs that offer competitive commissions, reliable payouts, and have a good reputation. Here are some of my favorite platforms that have helped me generate significant income:

1. **JVZoo**: Known for its wide range of digital products, JVZoo is a fantastic platform for affiliates who want to promote software, online courses, and digital marketing tools. The platform offers instant commissions and robust tracking features.

2. **ClickBank**: ClickBank specializes in digital products across various niches, from health and fitness to finance and self-improvement. It offers high commission rates and a vast marketplace of products to choose from. ClickBank's detailed analytics and affiliate tools make it easy to track performance and optimize campaigns.

3. **Warrior Plus**: Focused on internet marketing products, Warrior Plus is ideal for affiliates looking to promote tools and resources for online entrepreneurs. The platform provides detailed sales tracking, instant payments, and access to high-quality products.

Building a Platform for Affiliate Marketing

Creating a platform to share valuable content and incorporate affiliate links is crucial for success. Here are some popular platforms:

1. **Blog**: A blog is an excellent platform for affiliate marketing. By creating valuable content related to your niche, you can attract a targeted audience and incorporate affiliate links naturally. My blog, d-papa.com, is where I share my journey, tips, and reviews, helping others succeed in affiliate marketing.

2. **YouTube Channel**: Video content is highly engaging and can drive significant traffic. Create a YouTube channel to review products, provide tutorials, and share tips. Include affiliate links in your video descriptions and encourage viewers to check them out. *(Check out my YouTube channel for inspiration and more free training by visiting YouTube.com/dpapa)*

3. **Social Media**: Platforms like Instagram, Facebook, and Pinterest are great for promoting affiliate products. Share engaging content, use relevant hashtags, and include affiliate links in your posts or bio.

4. **Email List**: Building an email list allows you to communicate directly with your audience. Offer valuable content and product recommendations, and include affiliate links in your emails.

Effective Marketing Strategies

To succeed in affiliate marketing, you need to employ effective marketing strategies that drive traffic and conversions. Here are some key strategies:

1. **Content Marketing**: Create high-quality, valuable content that attracts and engages your target audience. This could be blog posts, videos, podcasts, or social media content. Focus on providing solutions to your audience's problems and naturally incorporate affiliate links.

2. **Search Engine Optimization (SEO)**: Optimize your content for search engines to increase visibility and drive organic traffic. Use relevant keywords, create high-quality backlinks, and ensure your website is user-friendly. SEO is a long-term strategy but can drive consistent, targeted traffic.

3. **Social Media Engagement**: Use social media platforms to promote your affiliate products and engage with your audience. Share valuable content, use engaging visuals, and interact with your followers. Paid advertising on social media can also be highly effective.

4. **Email Marketing**: Build and nurture an email list by offering valuable content and lead magnets. Send regular newsletters with product recommendations, exclusive deals, and valuable tips. Personalized and targeted emails can drive high conversion rates.

5. **Paid Advertising**: Invest in paid advertising to drive targeted traffic to your affiliate links. Use platforms like Google Ads,

Facebook Ads, and Instagram Ads. Start with a small budget, test different ads, and optimize based on performance.

Transparency and Trust

Building trust with your audience is crucial in affiliate marketing. Here's how to maintain transparency and foster trust:

1. **Disclosure**: Always disclose your affiliate relationships. Transparency builds trust with your audience and is also a legal requirement in many jurisdictions. Include a disclosure statement on your website and within your content.

2. **Honest Reviews**: Provide honest and unbiased reviews of the products you promote. Highlight both the pros and cons, and share your personal experience. Authenticity resonates with your audience and builds credibility.

3. **Value First**: Focus on providing value to your audience. Offer solutions, tips, and insights that genuinely help them. When your audience sees you as a valuable resource, they are more likely to trust your recommendations and click on your affiliate links.

Continuous Optimization

Affiliate marketing is a dynamic field that requires continuous optimization. Here's how to optimize your strategies for better performance:

1. **Track Performance**: Use analytics tools to track the performance of your affiliate links. Monitor metrics such as click-through rates, conversion rates, and earnings. Platforms like JVZoo, ClickBank, and Warrior Plus provide detailed analytics to help you track and optimize your campaigns.

2. **A/B Testing**: Conduct A/B testing to compare different versions of your content, ads, and emails. Test various headlines, calls to action, and visuals to determine what works best. Use the insights to refine your strategies and improve performance.

3. **Update Content**: Regularly update your content to keep it relevant and valuable. Update product reviews, add new insights, and refresh old content. This not only improves SEO but also keeps your audience engaged.

4. **Stay Informed**: Stay updated with the latest trends and best practices in affiliate marketing. Follow industry blogs, join affiliate marketing forums, and attend webinars or conferences. Continuous learning helps you stay ahead of the competition.

My Journey in Affiliate Marketing

My journey in affiliate marketing has been both challenging and rewarding. Through dedication and continuous learning, I've been able to generate significant income. Here are some highlights and tips from my journey:

1. **Starting with Passion**: I started my affiliate marketing journey by choosing niches I was passionate about, such as digital marketing and online entrepreneurship. This passion fueled my content creation and helped me connect with my audience.

2. **Building d-papa.com**: My blog, d-papa.com, has been a cornerstone of my affiliate marketing success. By sharing my journey, tips, and reviews, I've been able to attract a targeted audience and build trust. Consistent content creation and SEO have driven organic traffic to my blog.

3. **Leveraging Platforms**: I've leveraged platforms like JVZoo, ClickBank, and Warrior Plus to find high-quality products to promote. These platforms offer robust tools and resources that have helped me track performance and optimize my campaigns.

4. **Engaging Content**: Creating engaging and valuable content has been key to my success. Whether it's blog posts, videos, or social media content, I focus on providing solutions and genuine recommendations to my audience.

5. **Continuous Optimization**: I continuously track and optimize my strategies. From A/B testing ads to updating old content, I

ensure that my efforts are always improving. This continuous optimization has been crucial in achieving consistent results.

Real-Life Examples of Successful Affiliate Marketing Campaigns

Learning from real-life examples can provide valuable insights and inspiration. Here are some case studies of successful affiliate marketing campaigns:

1. **Fitness Blog Success**: John started a fitness blog focusing on weight loss and muscle building. He joined affiliate programs for fitness supplements, workout gear, and online training programs. By creating detailed product reviews, workout plans, and nutrition tips, John built a loyal audience. His blog's SEO and email marketing strategies drove significant traffic, resulting in an average monthly income of $8,000.

2. **YouTube Tech Channel**: Sarah launched a YouTube channel reviewing tech gadgets and software. She joined affiliate programs on platforms like JVZoo and ClickBank, promoting tools and products relevant to her audience. By providing honest reviews, tutorials, and unboxing videos, Sarah grew her subscriber base. Her engaging content and effective use of affiliate links in video descriptions led to an average monthly income of $12,000.

3. **Social Media Influencer**: Mark, a social media influencer in the travel niche, leveraged Instagram to promote travel gear, booking platforms, and travel insurance. By sharing stunning travel photos, engaging stories, and useful travel tips, Mark attracted a large following. Collaborations with brands and strategic use of affiliate links in posts and bio drove significant commissions, resulting in an average monthly income of $10,000.

Tools and Resources for Affiliate Marketers

Utilizing the right tools and resources can enhance your affiliate marketing strategy. Here are some valuable tools to consider:

1. **Analytics Tools**: Google Analytics, ClickMeter, and Bitly help track the performance of your affiliate links and campaigns. These tools provide insights into traffic sources, click-through rates, and conversions.

2. **SEO Tools**: Tools like Ahrefs, SEMrush, and Moz help optimize your content for search engines. They provide keyword research, backlink analysis, and site audit features to improve your SEO strategy.

3. **Content Creation Tools**: Canva for graphics, Grammarly for writing, and VidIQ for video optimization can enhance your content creation process. High-quality content drives engagement and conversions.

4. **Email Marketing Tools**: Platforms like Mailchimp, ConvertKit, and GetResponse help manage your email list, create campaigns, and track performance. Effective email marketing can drive significant traffic and sales.

5. **Social Media Management Tools**: Hootsuite, Buffer, and Later help schedule and manage your social media posts. Consistent social media engagement can boost your reach and affiliate income.

Building a Sustainable Affiliate Marketing Business

Building a sustainable affiliate marketing business requires more than just initial efforts. Here's how to ensure long-term success:

1. **Consistent Content Creation**: Regularly create and publish valuable content to keep your audience engaged and attract new visitors. Consistency is key to building a loyal audience and driving traffic.

2. **Building Relationships**: Build relationships with your audience, other affiliates, and product creators. Networking can lead to collaborations, exclusive deals, and new opportunities.

3. **Diversifying Income Streams**: Don't rely solely on one affiliate program or platform. Diversify your income streams

by promoting products from different programs and exploring new niches.

4. **Adapting to Changes**: Stay adaptable and be ready to pivot your strategies based on market trends and audience preferences. The affiliate marketing landscape is dynamic, and staying flexible ensures continued success.

5. **Investing in Learning**: Continuously invest in learning and improving your skills. Take courses, attend webinars, and read industry blogs to stay updated with the latest trends and best practices.

Affiliate marketing offers a powerful way to generate significant income by promoting products and services you believe in.

By choosing the right niche, selecting quality affiliate programs, and employing effective marketing strategies, you can build a sustainable and profitable affiliate marketing business.

Transparency, continuous optimization, and providing value to your audience are key to long-term success.

My journey in affiliate marketing, documented on d-papa.com, has shown that with dedication and the right approach, achieving a monthly income of $5,000 to $10,000 is entirely possible.

Chapter 7: Blogging and Content Creation

Blogging has evolved into a highly profitable venture, where high-quality content can attract a significant and loyal audience. In 2024, blogging offers numerous opportunities to generate substantial income, provided you approach it with the right strategies. Let's dive into the world of blogging, from setting up your blog to monetizing it effectively, and explore how you can replicate my success with my course, Flip Flop Profits, designed to teach you how to blog and monetize your blog for money.

Understanding the Power of Blogging

Blogging is more than just sharing your thoughts online; it's about creating valuable content that resonates with your audience, establishes your authority, and drives traffic to your site. A successful blog can generate income through various monetization strategies, turning your passion into a profitable business.

Starting Your Blog

Starting a blog involves several key steps to ensure you set a strong foundation for success:

1. **Selecting a Niche**: Choosing the right niche is crucial. Your niche should align with your interests and expertise, and have sufficient audience demand. Consider niches like health and fitness, personal finance, travel, technology, or digital marketing. Research your potential audience's needs and preferences using tools like Google Trends and keyword research.

2. **Setting Up a Domain and Hosting**: Once you've chosen your niche, select a domain name that reflects your blog's focus and is easy to remember. Use reliable hosting services like Bluehost, SiteGround, or WP Engine to ensure your blog is fast and secure. A good hosting service can enhance your site's performance and user experience.

3. **Designing an Appealing Layout**: An attractive, user-friendly layout can significantly impact your blog's success. Use content management systems (CMS) like WordPress, which offer customizable themes and plugins. Focus on a clean, responsive design that looks good on all devices. Include easy navigation, a clear call to action, and an intuitive user interface.

Creating High-Quality Content

Content is the heart of your blog. Creating high-quality, valuable content that engages your audience and drives traffic is essential. Here's how to create compelling content:

1. **Identify Your Audience's Needs**: Understand what your audience is looking for and create content that addresses their

needs. Use tools like Google Analytics and social media insights to gather information about your audience's interests and preferences.

2. **Content Planning**: Develop a content plan that outlines the topics you'll cover, the type of content (e.g., blog posts, videos, infographics), and a posting schedule. Consistency is key, so plan your content in advance and stick to a regular posting schedule.

3. **Writing Engaging Posts**: Write in a conversational tone, as if you're speaking directly to your readers. Use clear, concise language and break up your text with subheadings, bullet points, and images to make it more readable. Incorporate storytelling to make your content more relatable and engaging.

4. **SEO Optimization**: Optimize your content for search engines to improve visibility and drive organic traffic. Use relevant keywords, meta descriptions, and high-quality backlinks. Ensure your content is well-structured, with proper headings (H1, H2, H3) and alt text for images.

5. **Multimedia Integration**: Enhance your content with multimedia elements like images, videos, infographics, and podcasts. These elements can make your content more engaging and appealing, catering to different audience preferences.

Monetization Strategies

Turning your blog into a substantial income source involves implementing effective monetization strategies. Here are some popular methods:

1. **Advertising**: Display ads through networks like Google AdSense or Media.net can generate revenue based on impressions or clicks. Place ads strategically on your blog to maximize visibility without compromising user experience.

2. **Affiliate Marketing**: Promote products or services through affiliate links and earn a commission for every sale made

through your links. Choose affiliate programs that align with your niche and audience. Platforms like JVZoo, ClickBank, and Warrior Plus offer a wide range of affiliate products.

3. **Sponsored Posts**: Collaborate with brands to create sponsored content. Brands pay you to write posts that promote their products or services. Ensure the sponsored content aligns with your blog's theme and provides value to your audience.

4. **Selling Products or Services**: Create and sell your own digital or physical products. This could include ebooks, online courses, merchandise, or consulting services. My course, Flip Flop Profits, is an example of a product that teaches others how to blog and monetize their blog for money.

5. **Membership and Subscription Models**: Offer premium content or exclusive access to a membership area for a subscription fee. This model works well for in-depth tutorials, community access, or premium resources.

Consistency and Engagement

Consistency in posting and engagement with your readers are crucial for growing your blog. Here's how to maintain consistency and foster engagement:

1. **Regular Posting Schedule**: Stick to a consistent posting schedule to keep your audience engaged and coming back for more. Whether it's weekly, bi-weekly, or monthly, consistency builds trust and anticipation among your readers.

2. **Reader Interaction**: Engage with your readers by responding to comments, emails, and social media interactions. Ask questions, invite feedback, and create a sense of community. Engaging with your audience builds loyalty and encourages repeat visits.

3. **Social Media Leverage**: Use social media platforms to promote your content and interact with your audience. Share your blog posts, create engaging social media content, and

participate in relevant groups or forums. Social media can drive significant traffic to your blog and expand your reach.

Leveraging Social Media

Social media is a powerful tool for promoting your blog and driving traffic. Here's how to effectively leverage social media:

1. **Platform Selection**: Choose the right social media platforms based on your audience and niche. For example, Instagram and Pinterest are great for visual content, while Twitter and LinkedIn work well for professional or news-related content.

2. **Content Sharing**: Share your blog posts and related content on social media. Use eye-catching visuals, compelling headlines, and relevant hashtags to increase visibility and engagement.

3. **Engagement and Interaction**: Actively engage with your followers by responding to comments, participating in conversations, and sharing user-generated content. Building relationships with your audience on social media can drive traffic and enhance loyalty.

4. **Paid Advertising**: Invest in paid social media advertising to reach a larger audience. Platforms like Facebook Ads, Instagram Ads, and Pinterest Ads offer targeted advertising options that can drive traffic to your blog and increase visibility.

Building a Community

Building a community around your blog can enhance reader engagement and foster loyalty. Here's how to build a strong community:

1. **Encourage Comments**: Invite readers to leave comments on your blog posts. Respond to their comments to create a dialogue and show that you value their input.

2. **Create a Forum or Group**: Create a forum or a social media group where your readers can interact with each other and

discuss topics related to your niche. This can create a sense of community and encourage regular engagement.

3. **Host Webinars and Live Sessions**: Host webinars, live Q&A sessions, or online workshops to interact with your audience in real-time. These sessions can provide additional value to your readers and strengthen your community.

Using Flip Flop Profits to Teach Blogging and Monetization

To help others succeed in blogging and monetization, I've created a comprehensive course called Flip Flop Profits. Here's what you can expect from the course:

1. **Comprehensive Training**: Flip Flop Profits offers in-depth training on every aspect of blogging, from setting up your blog to creating high-quality content and implementing monetization strategies. It's designed for both beginners and experienced bloggers looking to refine their skills.

2. **Practical Resources**: The course includes practical resources like templates, checklists, and tools that streamline the blogging process. These resources save you time and ensure you don't miss any critical steps.

3. **Community Support**: Join a community of like-minded bloggers who share their experiences, offer support, and provide valuable feedback. Networking with others can lead to collaborations and new opportunities.

4. **Expert Guidance**: Learn from my experience and insights. I share tips, strategies, and best practices that have helped me build and monetize successful blogs.

5. **Continuous Updates**: Blogging trends and best practices evolve, and Flip Flop Profits provides regular updates to keep you informed about the latest strategies and tools.

Measuring Success

Tracking your blog's performance is essential to understand what's working and where you can improve. Here are some key metrics to monitor:

1. **Traffic**: Use tools like Google Analytics to track your blog's traffic. Monitor metrics like page views, unique visitors, and bounce rate to understand your audience's behavior and the effectiveness of your content.

2. **Engagement**: Measure engagement metrics such as comments, shares, and time spent on your site. High engagement indicates that your content resonates with your audience.

3. **Conversion Rates**: Track conversion rates for your monetization strategies. This includes affiliate link clicks, ad impressions, product sales, and email sign-ups. Understanding conversion rates helps you optimize your strategies for better results.

4. **Revenue**: Monitor your blog's revenue from various monetization sources. This includes ad revenue, affiliate commissions, sponsored posts, and product sales. Regularly review your earnings to identify trends and opportunities for growth.

Overcoming Challenges in Blogging

Blogging comes with its own set of challenges. Here's how to overcome some common obstacles:

1. **Content Burnout**: Creating consistent, high-quality content can be demanding. Plan your content in advance, use content calendars, and take breaks when needed to avoid burnout. Collaborate with guest bloggers or outsource content creation to manage workload.

2. **Increasing Competition**: The blogging landscape is competitive. Differentiate your blog by offering unique value, high-quality content, and a compelling brand story. Focus on building a loyal audience rather than competing solely on traffic.

3. **Monetization Struggles**: Monetizing a blog can take time and effort. Experiment with different monetization strategies, track their performance, and optimize based on results. Diversify your income streams to reduce reliance on a single source.

4. **Technical Issues**: Technical issues like website downtime, slow loading speeds, or security breaches can affect your blog's performance. Use reliable hosting services, regularly update your software, and implement security measures to mitigate these issues.

5. **Maintaining Motivation**: Blogging is a long-term commitment, and maintaining motivation can be challenging. Set realistic goals, celebrate small wins, and stay focused on your long-term vision. Surround yourself with a supportive community to stay motivated.

Future Trends in Blogging

Staying ahead of future trends can give you a competitive edge in the blogging world. Here are some trends to watch in 2024:

1. **Voice Search Optimization**: With the rise of voice assistants, optimizing your content for voice search can enhance visibility. Focus on natural language, long-tail keywords, and concise answers to common questions.

2. **Video Content**: Video content continues to gain popularity. Incorporate videos into your blog, create a YouTube channel, and engage with your audience through live sessions and webinars.

3. **Personalization**: Personalized content tailored to individual preferences can significantly enhance user experience. Use data and analytics to understand your audience and create personalized content and recommendations.

4. **Interactive Content**: Interactive elements like quizzes, polls, and infographics can boost engagement. Incorporate interactive content into your blog to create a more immersive experience for your audience.

5. **Sustainability**: There's a growing emphasis on sustainability and ethical practices. Highlight your commitment to sustainability in your content and business practices to attract socially conscious readers.

Blogging and content creation offer powerful opportunities to build a substantial income source.

By selecting the right niche, creating high-quality content, and implementing effective monetization strategies, you can turn your blog into a profitable venture.

Consistency, engagement, and continuous optimization are key to long-term success.

My journey in blogging, documented on d-papa.com, and my course, Flip Flop Profits, provide a roadmap for aspiring bloggers to achieve financial independence.

Chapter 8: Online Tutoring and Course Creation

The rise of e-learning has revolutionized education, creating vast opportunities for online educators. Whether you're an expert in a particular field or have a passion for teaching, the digital landscape offers a platform to share your knowledge and generate significant income. Let's explore how to identify your niche, choose the right platform, create engaging content, and effectively market your courses for long-term success.

Understanding the Power of E-Learning

E-learning has become a cornerstone of modern education, providing flexibility, accessibility, and a personalized learning experience. With the proliferation of high-speed internet and advanced technology, online tutoring and course creation have become viable and lucrative career options.

Identifying Your Niche

Choosing the right niche is the first and most crucial step in online tutoring and course creation. Here's how to identify a profitable and fulfilling niche:

1. **Passion and Expertise**: Select a niche that you are passionate about and have substantial knowledge in. Your enthusiasm will translate into your teaching, making your courses more engaging and authentic.

2. **Market Demand**: Conduct market research to identify the demand for your chosen niche. Use tools like Google Trends, keyword research, and competitor analysis to gauge interest and competition. Look for niches with a significant audience and unmet needs.

3. **Target Audience**: Define your target audience. Understand their demographics, preferences, and pain points. Tailor your content to address their specific needs and challenges.

Choosing the Right Platform

Selecting the right platform is essential for delivering your courses effectively and reaching a broader audience. Here are some popular platforms to consider:

1. **Udemy**: Udemy is one of the largest online learning marketplaces, offering a vast audience and robust tools for course creation. It's ideal for reaching a global audience and leveraging Udemy's marketing capabilities.

2. **Teachable**: Teachable allows you to create and sell your courses on a customizable platform. It offers comprehensive tools for course creation, student management, and payment processing. Teachable is great for building a branded online school.

3. **Thinkific**: Thinkific provides an all-in-one platform for creating, marketing, and selling online courses. It offers customization options, marketing tools, and seamless integration with other software.

4. **Kajabi**: Kajabi is a premium platform that combines course creation with marketing automation, email campaigns, and membership sites. It's perfect for entrepreneurs looking to build a comprehensive online business.

Creating Engaging Content

The success of your online courses hinges on creating engaging and valuable content that enhances the learning experience. Here's how to create content that captivates your audience:

1. **Course Planning**: Start with a detailed course outline. Define the learning objectives, key topics, and structure of your course. Break down the content into manageable modules and lessons. Planning ensures a coherent and logical flow.

2. **Video Lectures**: Video content is highly engaging and effective for teaching. Invest in good quality recording equipment, including a camera, microphone, and lighting. Create professional-looking videos by scripting your content, using clear visuals, and maintaining a steady pace.

3. **Interactive Assignments**: Include interactive assignments to reinforce learning. These could be quizzes, exercises, projects, or discussion prompts. Interactive elements keep students engaged and provide opportunities for practical application.

4. **Quizzes and Assessments**: Regular quizzes and assessments help evaluate student progress and understanding. Use a mix of multiple-choice, short-answer, and practical questions. Provide feedback to guide students and address any learning gaps.

5. **Supplementary Materials**: Enhance your courses with supplementary materials like slides, PDFs, and additional reading resources. These materials provide additional value and help students grasp complex concepts.

Monetizing Your Courses

Monetizing your online courses involves several strategies to generate significant income. Here's how to effectively monetize your courses:

1. **Direct Sales**: Sell your courses directly to students on platforms like Udemy or your website. Set competitive pricing based on the value and depth of your content. Offer discounts or promotions to attract new students.

2. **Subscription Models**: Offer a subscription model where students pay a recurring fee for access to all your courses. This model provides steady and predictable income. Platforms like Teachable and Kajabi support subscription-based pricing.

3. **Corporate Training**: Partner with companies to provide corporate training solutions. Tailor your courses to meet the specific needs of businesses and offer bulk enrollment discounts. Corporate training can be a lucrative revenue stream.

4. **Membership Sites**: Create a membership site where students pay a monthly or annual fee for exclusive access to courses, resources, and community support. Membership sites build a loyal student base and generate recurring revenue.

5. **Bundling Courses**: Bundle multiple courses together and offer them at a discounted rate. Bundling provides more value to students and can increase overall sales.

Effective Marketing Strategies

Marketing is crucial for attracting students and growing your online course business. Here are some effective marketing strategies:

1. **Content Marketing**: Create valuable content related to your niche to attract and engage your audience. This could be blog posts, videos, podcasts, or social media content. Share insights, tips, and free resources to build trust and authority.

2. **Email Marketing**: Build an email list to communicate directly with your audience. Offer a free lead magnet, such as an ebook

or mini-course, in exchange for email sign-ups. Send regular newsletters with course updates, promotions, and valuable content.

3. **Social Media Marketing**: Use social media platforms to promote your courses and engage with your audience. Share engaging content, use relevant hashtags, and participate in relevant groups or discussions. Paid social media advertising can also be highly effective.

4. **Search Engine Optimization (SEO)**: Optimize your website and course pages for search engines to increase visibility and drive organic traffic. Use relevant keywords, create high-quality backlinks, and ensure your content is well-structured.

5. **Partnerships and Collaborations**: Partner with other educators, influencers, or businesses in your niche to expand your reach. Collaborate on webinars, guest posts, or joint ventures to attract new students.

Continuous Content Updates

Keeping your courses up-to-date is essential for maintaining their relevance and value. Here's how to ensure your content remains current:

1. **Regular Reviews**: Regularly review your course content to identify outdated information or areas that need improvement. Update your content based on new developments, feedback, and industry trends.

2. **Student Feedback**: Encourage students to provide feedback on your courses. Use this feedback to make necessary updates and improvements. Positive reviews and testimonials can also enhance your course's credibility.

3. **Add New Content**: Continuously add new content to your courses. This could be new modules, updated resources, or bonus materials. Keeping your courses fresh and valuable encourages repeat enrollments and student retention.

4. **Monitor Industry Trends**: Stay informed about the latest trends and developments in your niche. Incorporate new knowledge, tools, and techniques into your courses to ensure they remain relevant and cutting-edge.

Staying Current with E-Learning Trends

The e-learning landscape is constantly evolving. Staying current with the latest trends and best practices is crucial for long-term success. Here are some trends to watch in 2024:

1. **Microlearning**: Microlearning involves breaking down content into small, digestible chunks. This approach caters to busy learners and enhances retention. Incorporate microlearning elements into your courses to improve engagement.

2. **Gamification**: Gamification uses game elements, such as points, badges, and leaderboards, to motivate and engage learners. Adding gamified elements to your courses can make learning more interactive and enjoyable.

3. **Artificial Intelligence (AI)**: AI can personalize the learning experience by adapting content based on individual progress and preferences. Explore AI-powered tools to enhance your course delivery and student engagement.

4. **Virtual Reality (VR) and Augmented Reality (AR)**: VR and AR technologies provide immersive learning experiences. Incorporate VR or AR elements into your courses to offer hands-on, experiential learning.

5. **Mobile Learning**: Ensure your courses are mobile-friendly, as more learners prefer accessing content on their smartphones and tablets. Optimize your course design and content for mobile devices.

Case Studies of Successful Online Educators

Learning from successful online educators can provide valuable insights and inspiration. Here are some case studies:

1. **Language Learning Course**: Maria created an online Spanish language course on Udemy. By offering high-quality video lessons, interactive exercises, and cultural insights, she attracted thousands of students. Her focus on engagement and practical application resulted in an average monthly income of $5,000.

2. **Digital Marketing Academy**: John launched a digital marketing academy on Teachable. He offered comprehensive courses on SEO, social media marketing, and PPC advertising. By leveraging content marketing, SEO, and partnerships, John built a loyal student base and generated over $10,000 per month.

3. **Fitness and Wellness Platform**: Sarah developed a fitness and wellness platform using Thinkific. She provided workout videos, nutrition plans, and mental wellness resources. By offering a subscription model and corporate wellness programs, Sarah's platform became a significant income source, earning her $8,000 monthly.

Tools and Resources for Course Creation

Utilizing the right tools and resources can enhance your course creation process. Here are some valuable tools to consider:

1. **Video Recording and Editing**: Tools like Camtasia, ScreenFlow, and Adobe Premiere Pro can help you create professional-quality video lectures. These tools offer recording, editing, and screen capture features.

2. **Presentation Software**: Use PowerPoint, Keynote, or Google Slides to create engaging presentations for your courses. Combine slides with your video lectures to enhance the learning experience.

3. **Learning Management Systems (LMS)**: Platforms like Moodle, Blackboard, and Canvas provide comprehensive LMS solutions for course creation, student management, and content delivery.

4. **Assessment Tools**: Use tools like Typeform, Google Forms, and Quizlet to create interactive quizzes and assessments. These tools help evaluate student progress and provide valuable feedback.

5. **Email Marketing Tools**: Platforms like Mailchimp, ConvertKit, and GetResponse help manage your email list, create campaigns, and track performance. Effective email marketing can drive enrollments and engagement.

Building a Sustainable Online Course Business

Building a sustainable online course business requires more than just creating and selling courses. Here's how to ensure long-term success:

1. **Consistent Content Creation**: Regularly create and update your courses to keep them relevant and valuable. Consistency in content creation builds trust and keeps your audience engaged.

2. **Building Relationships**: Foster strong relationships with your students. Engage with them through comments, emails, and social media. Offer support and additional resources to enhance their learning experience.

3. **Diversifying Income Streams**: Don't rely solely on one course or platform. Diversify your income streams by offering multiple courses, corporate training, and membership models. Explore different niches and audience segments.

4. **Adapting to Changes**: Stay adaptable and be ready to pivot your strategies based on market trends and student feedback. The e-learning landscape is dynamic, and staying flexible ensures continued success.

5. **Investing in Learning**: Continuously invest in learning and improving your skills. Take courses, attend webinars, and read industry blogs to stay updated with the latest trends and best practices.

Overcoming Challenges in Online Tutoring and Course Creation

Online tutoring and course creation come with their own set of challenges. Here's how to overcome some common obstacles:

1. **Content Creation Burnout**: Creating consistent, high-quality content can be demanding. Plan your content in advance, use content calendars, and take breaks when needed to avoid burnout. Collaborate with guest instructors or outsource content creation to manage workload.

2. **Increasing Competition**: The e-learning landscape is competitive. Differentiate your courses by offering unique value, high-quality content, and a compelling brand story. Focus on building a loyal student base rather than competing solely on price.

3. **Monetization Struggles**: Monetizing courses can take time and effort. Experiment with different monetization strategies, track their performance, and optimize based on results. Diversify your income streams to reduce reliance on a single source.

4. **Technical Issues**: Technical issues like website downtime, slow loading speeds, or security breaches can affect your course delivery. Use reliable hosting services, regularly update your software, and implement security measures to mitigate these issues.

5. **Maintaining Motivation**: Building a successful online course business is a long-term commitment, and maintaining motivation can be challenging. Set realistic goals, celebrate small wins, and stay focused on your long-term vision. Surround yourself with a supportive community to stay motivated.

Future Trends in E-Learning

Staying ahead of future trends can give you a competitive edge in the e-learning industry. Here are some trends to watch in 2024:

1. **Personalized Learning**: Personalized learning experiences tailored to individual preferences and progress can enhance student engagement and outcomes. Use data and AI to create personalized content and recommendations.

2. **Blended Learning**: Blended learning combines online and offline learning experiences. Incorporate live sessions, group discussions, and hands-on activities into your courses to offer a more holistic learning experience.

3. **Sustainability and Social Impact**: There's a growing emphasis on sustainability and social impact in education. Highlight your commitment to sustainability in your content and business practices to attract socially conscious students.

4. **Lifelong Learning**: The demand for lifelong learning is increasing. Offer courses that cater to continuous professional development and personal growth. Focus on skills that are in high demand and relevant to evolving job markets.

5. **Global Reach**: The e-learning market is expanding globally. Create courses that cater to international students, offer multilingual content, and adapt to different cultural contexts. Expanding your reach can open up new opportunities and revenue streams.

Online tutoring and course creation offer powerful opportunities to share your knowledge, impact lives, and generate substantial income. By identifying the right niche, creating engaging content, and implementing effective monetization and marketing strategies, you can build a successful and sustainable online course business.

My journey in e-learning has shown that with dedication and the right approach, achieving significant income and making a positive impact is entirely possible.

Chapter 9: Print on Demand Business

The print on demand (POD) business model has revolutionized the way we sell customized products, enabling entrepreneurs to launch businesses without the need for holding inventory. With POD, you can create and sell products with unique designs, from t-shirts and mugs to posters and phone cases, all without upfront costs or logistical headaches. Let's explore how to set up a successful POD business, from choosing a niche and platform to marketing strategies and maintaining excellent customer service.

Understanding the Print on Demand Model

Print on demand (POD) is a business model where products are only printed once an order is placed, allowing you to sell customized merchandise without maintaining inventory. This model minimizes risk and initial investment, making it accessible for entrepreneurs at any stage. The POD provider handles the printing, packaging, and shipping, allowing you to focus on designing and marketing your products.

Benefits of Print on Demand

1. **Low Startup Costs**: With no need to purchase inventory upfront, the initial investment is minimal. You only pay for the product once a sale is made.
2. **Wide Product Range**: POD platforms offer a wide variety of products you can customize and sell, including apparel, accessories, home decor, and more.
3. **Scalability**: Since you're not handling inventory or fulfillment, you can easily scale your business as demand grows.
4. **Creative Freedom**: Focus on creating unique designs that resonate with your target audience without worrying about production logistics.

Choosing a Niche

Selecting the right niche is crucial for the success of your POD business. Here's how to choose a niche that aligns with your interests and has market potential:

1. **Passion and Interests**: Choose a niche you're passionate about. Your enthusiasm will drive your creativity and marketing efforts. Whether it's fitness, pets, travel, or pop culture, select a niche you're excited about.

2. **Market Research**: Conduct thorough market research to identify niches with high demand and low competition. Use tools like Google Trends, keyword research, and competitor analysis to gauge interest and identify gaps in the market.

3. **Target Audience**: Define your target audience and understand their preferences, needs, and pain points. Tailor your designs and marketing strategies to appeal to this specific group.

Selecting a Platform

Choosing the right POD platform is essential for seamless operations and customer satisfaction. Here are some popular POD platforms to consider:

1. **Printful**: Printful is a leading POD provider offering a wide range of products, from apparel and accessories to home decor. It integrates with major e-commerce platforms like Shopify, WooCommerce, and Etsy, making it easy to manage your store.

2. **Teespring**: Teespring allows you to create and sell custom products with no upfront costs. It provides tools for designing, marketing, and selling your products directly through its platform or integrating with other e-commerce sites.

3. **Redbubble**: Redbubble is a marketplace for artists and designers to sell their work on various products. It's ideal for creatives who want to reach a broad audience without managing their own e-commerce site.

4. **Society6**: Society6 focuses on high-quality art and design products, from wall art to furniture. It's perfect for artists looking to showcase their designs on premium products.

Creating Unique Designs

Creating compelling and unique designs is the heart of a successful POD business. Here's how to create designs that resonate with your audience:

1. **Design Tools**: Use design software like Adobe Illustrator, Photoshop, or free tools like Canva to create your designs. These tools offer various features and templates to bring your creative ideas to life.

2. **Trends and Inspiration**: Stay updated with design trends and seek inspiration from popular styles and themes in your niche. Platforms like Pinterest, Instagram, and design blogs are great for finding inspiration.

3. **Originality**: Ensure your designs are original and stand out from the competition. Avoid copying other designers' work and focus on creating unique designs that reflect your brand's personality.

4. **Feedback and Testing**: Gather feedback from your target audience before finalizing your designs. Use social media polls, surveys, or focus groups to understand what resonates with your audience. Testing different designs can help you identify what works best.

Setting Up Your Online Store

Setting up an online store is essential for selling your POD products. Here's how to get started:

1. **Choose an E-commerce Platform**: Select an e-commerce platform that integrates with your chosen POD provider. Shopify, WooCommerce, and BigCommerce are popular options that offer seamless integration with POD platforms.

2. **Domain and Branding**: Choose a memorable domain name that reflects your brand. Invest in professional branding, including a logo, color scheme, and overall design aesthetic that aligns with your niche and appeals to your target audience.

3. **Product Listings**: Create detailed and appealing product listings with high-quality images, compelling descriptions, and accurate pricing. Use mockup generators provided by POD platforms to showcase your products realistically.

4. **Payment and Shipping**: Set up secure payment gateways to accept payments from customers. Define your shipping policies, including shipping rates and delivery times, to set clear expectations for your customers.

Marketing Strategies

Effective marketing is crucial for driving traffic to your store and converting visitors into customers. Here are some key marketing strategies:

1. **Social Media Marketing**: Use social media platforms like Instagram, Facebook, and Pinterest to promote your products. Share engaging content, use relevant hashtags, and interact with your audience. Paid advertising on social media can also drive targeted traffic to your store.

2. **Influencer Collaborations**: Partner with influencers in your niche to reach a larger audience. Influencers can showcase your products to their followers, driving traffic and sales. Choose influencers whose audience aligns with your target market.

3. **Email Marketing**: Build an email list to communicate directly with your audience. Offer incentives like discounts or free downloads to encourage sign-ups. Send regular newsletters with product updates, promotions, and valuable content to keep your audience engaged.

4. **Content Marketing**: Create valuable content related to your niche to attract and engage your audience. This could be blog

posts, videos, or tutorials. Content marketing helps build trust and authority, driving organic traffic to your store.

5. **SEO Optimization**: Optimize your online store for search engines to increase visibility and drive organic traffic. Use relevant keywords, meta descriptions, and high-quality backlinks. Ensure your website is user-friendly and fast-loading.

Providing Excellent Customer Service

Excellent customer service is key to maintaining a positive reputation and encouraging repeat business. Here's how to provide top-notch customer service:

1. **Responsive Communication**: Respond to customer inquiries promptly and courteously. Provide clear and helpful information to address their questions and concerns. Use automated responses for common queries to ensure timely communication.

2. **Order Tracking**: Keep customers informed about their order status with automated tracking updates. Provide estimated delivery times and notify customers of any delays.

3. **Hassle-Free Returns**: Offer a clear and fair return policy to build trust with your customers. Make the return process simple and straightforward, and handle returns efficiently to ensure customer satisfaction.

4. **Customer Feedback**: Encourage customers to leave reviews and provide feedback. Use this feedback to improve your products and services. Positive reviews can enhance your store's credibility and attract new customers.

Quality Control

Maintaining high-quality standards is crucial for the success of your POD business. Here's how to ensure consistent quality:

1. **Sample Orders**: Regularly order samples of your products to check the print quality, materials, and overall appearance. This helps you identify any issues and make necessary adjustments.

2. **Reliable POD Provider**: Choose a POD provider with a reputation for high-quality products and reliable service. Read reviews, check their product catalog, and assess their production capabilities before partnering with them.

3. **Quality Checks**: Implement quality checks at various stages of the production process. Ensure your designs are correctly aligned, colors are accurate, and the final product meets your standards.

4. **Customer Satisfaction**: Monitor customer reviews and feedback to identify any quality issues. Address these issues promptly and take corrective actions to maintain high-quality standards.

Scaling Your POD Business

As your POD business grows, consider these strategies to scale effectively:

1. **Expand Product Range**: Introduce new products regularly to keep your offerings fresh and appealing. Conduct market research to identify trending products and add them to your catalog.

2. **Explore New Niches**: Diversify your product range by exploring new niches and target audiences. This can help you reach a broader market and increase sales.

3. **Invest in Marketing**: Increase your marketing budget to reach a larger audience. Use data from your existing campaigns to optimize your advertising efforts and maximize ROI.

4. **Automate Processes**: Use automation tools to streamline your operations, from order processing and customer communication to marketing and inventory management. Automation can save time and improve efficiency.

5. **Build a Team**: As your business grows, consider hiring additional staff or freelancers to handle customer service, design, marketing, and other tasks. Building a team allows you to focus on strategic growth and expansion.

Overcoming Challenges in POD

Running a POD business comes with its own set of challenges. Here's how to overcome some common obstacles:

1. **Design Consistency**: Maintaining design consistency across different products can be challenging. Use templates and design guidelines to ensure your designs look great on all products.

2. **Inventory Management**: Although POD eliminates the need for inventory, keeping track of product availability and production times is crucial. Work closely with your POD provider to manage inventory and avoid stockouts.

3. **Shipping Delays**: Shipping delays can negatively impact customer satisfaction. Set realistic delivery expectations and communicate any delays promptly. Work with reliable POD providers that offer efficient shipping options.

4. **Competitive Market**: The POD market is highly competitive. Differentiate your products by offering unique designs, high-quality materials, and exceptional customer service. Focus on building a strong brand and loyal customer base.

Future Trends in Print on Demand

Staying ahead of future trends can give you a competitive edge in the POD industry. Here are some trends to watch in 2024:

1. **Sustainable Products**: There's a growing demand for eco-friendly and sustainable products. Offer products made from organic, recycled, or sustainable materials to attract environmentally conscious customers.

2. **Personalization**: Personalized products are increasingly popular. Allow customers to customize their products with names, dates, or custom messages. Personalization can enhance customer satisfaction and drive repeat business.

3. **Augmented Reality (AR)**: AR technology can enhance the online shopping experience by allowing customers to visualize products in their environment before purchasing. Integrate AR features into your online store to provide an immersive shopping experience.

4. **Niche Marketplaces**: Niche-specific marketplaces are emerging, offering targeted platforms for unique products. Explore opportunities to list your products on niche marketplaces to reach a more specific audience.

5. **Direct-to-Consumer (DTC) Brands**: DTC brands are gaining traction, offering high-quality products directly to consumers without intermediaries. Focus on building a strong DTC brand with a loyal customer base.

Case Studies of Successful POD Businesses

Learning from successful POD businesses can provide valuable insights and inspiration. Here are some case studies:

1. **Apparel Brand**: Lisa launched a POD apparel brand focusing on fitness and motivational designs. By leveraging social media marketing and influencer collaborations, her brand quickly gained traction. Lisa's commitment to quality and customer service resulted in an average monthly income of $10,000.

2. **Art and Home Decor**: John, an artist, started selling his artwork on products like posters, canvas prints, and home decor items through Redbubble. His unique designs attracted a global audience, and by consistently updating his portfolio and engaging with customers, John built a successful POD business generating $7,000 per month.

3. **Niche Merchandise**: Sarah created a POD business selling pet-themed merchandise, including apparel and accessories for pet

owners. By targeting a passionate and specific audience, she built a loyal customer base. Sarah's focus on high-quality designs and excellent customer service helped her achieve a monthly income of $8,000.

Tools and Resources for POD Businesses

Utilizing the right tools and resources can enhance your POD business operations. Here are some valuable tools to consider:

1. **Design Software**: Use tools like Adobe Illustrator, Photoshop, or Canva for creating high-quality designs. These tools offer various features and templates to bring your creative ideas to life.

2. **E-commerce Platforms**: Shopify, WooCommerce, and BigCommerce provide robust e-commerce solutions for managing your online store. These platforms integrate seamlessly with POD providers and offer various customization options.

3. **Marketing Tools**: Tools like Hootsuite, Buffer, and Later help schedule and manage your social media posts. Email marketing platforms like Mailchimp, ConvertKit, and GetResponse help build and manage your email list.

4. **Analytics Tools**: Google Analytics, Facebook Insights, and Shopify Analytics provide valuable insights into your store's performance. Use these tools to track traffic, sales, and customer behavior to optimize your strategies.

5. **Customer Service Tools**: Use tools like Zendesk, Freshdesk, or Help Scout to manage customer inquiries and provide excellent support. These tools help streamline communication and enhance customer satisfaction.

Building a Sustainable POD Business

Building a sustainable POD business requires more than just creating and selling products. Here's how to ensure long-term success:

6. **Consistent Quality**: Maintain consistent quality in your products and designs. Regularly review and update your offerings to meet customer expectations and industry standards.

7. **Building Relationships**: Foster strong relationships with your customers. Engage with them through social media, email marketing, and personalized communication. Loyal customers are more likely to make repeat purchases and recommend your brand.

8. **Diversifying Income Streams**: Don't rely solely on one product or platform. Diversify your income streams by offering various products, exploring new niches, and expanding to different marketplaces.

9. **Adapting to Changes**: Stay adaptable and be ready to pivot your strategies based on market trends and customer feedback. The POD industry is dynamic, and staying flexible ensures continued success.

10. **Investing in Learning**: Continuously invest in learning and improving your skills. Take courses, attend webinars, and read industry blogs to stay updated with the latest trends and best practices.

The print on demand business model offers a unique opportunity to sell customized products without the hassle of inventory management. By choosing the right niche, creating unique designs, and implementing effective marketing strategies, you can build a profitable and sustainable POD business. Excellent customer service and regular quality control are key to maintaining a positive reputation and encouraging repeat business.

My journey in POD has shown that with dedication and the right approach, achieving significant income and making a positive impact is entirely possible. I worked close with Gearbubble, and was able to achieve great results, which made me teach others with GB Cracked (https://www.d-papa.com/gbcracked) which I released back in 2016 on Jvzoo.

Chapter 10: Mobile App Development

Developing mobile apps can be a highly profitable endeavor, offering vast opportunities to reach millions of users worldwide. The process involves validating your app idea, designing a user-friendly interface, developing the app using appropriate technologies, and implementing effective monetization strategies. In this chapter, we will explore the key steps to successful mobile app development, from concept to post-launch, and how to maintain and grow your app's user base and income.

Understanding the Potential of Mobile App Development

Mobile apps have become an integral part of our daily lives, providing solutions for various needs, from entertainment and social networking to productivity and health. The mobile app market continues to grow, driven by the increasing adoption of smartphones and tablets. Developing a successful mobile app can lead to substantial financial rewards and the ability to impact users on a global scale.

Validating Your App Idea

Before diving into development, it's essential to validate your app idea to ensure there is a market demand and that your app provides a unique solution. Here's how to validate your app idea:

1. **Market Research**: Conduct thorough market research to understand the demand for your app idea. Analyze existing apps in your niche, identify their strengths and weaknesses, and find gaps your app can fill. Use tools like App Annie, Sensor Tower, and Google Trends to gather data on app performance and market trends.

2. **Target Audience**: Define your target audience and understand their needs, preferences, and pain points. Create user personas to visualize your ideal users and tailor your app's features to meet their requirements.

3. **Competitive Analysis**: Analyze your competitors' apps to understand what they offer and how you can differentiate your app. Identify opportunities to provide a better user experience, additional features, or improved performance.

4. **Minimum Viable Product (MVP)**: Develop a minimum viable product (MVP) with the core features of your app. Launching an MVP allows you to test your idea with real users, gather feedback, and make necessary adjustments before investing in full-scale development.

Designing a User-Friendly Interface

A user-friendly interface is crucial for the success of your mobile app. It enhances user experience, encourages engagement, and increases retention rates. Here's how to design an intuitive and appealing interface:

1. **User-Centered Design**: Focus on creating a design that meets the needs and preferences of your target audience. Conduct user research, usability testing, and gather feedback to inform your design decisions.

2. **Simplicity and Clarity**: Keep the interface simple and uncluttered. Use clear and concise language, intuitive navigation, and minimalistic design elements. Avoid overwhelming users with too many features or complex interactions.

3. **Consistent Design Language**: Maintain consistency in design elements such as colors, fonts, buttons, and icons. Consistent design creates a cohesive user experience and helps users navigate your app more easily.

4. **Responsive Design**: Ensure your app is responsive and performs well on various devices and screen sizes. Test your app on different devices to identify and fix any layout or performance issues.

5. **Accessibility**: Design your app to be accessible to all users, including those with disabilities. Follow accessibility guidelines and best practices to ensure your app is usable by a diverse audience.

Developing Your Mobile App

Once you have validated your idea and designed a user-friendly interface, it's time to develop your mobile app. Here's a step-by-step guide to the development process:

1. **Choose the Right Technology Stack**: Select the appropriate technologies for your app based on your requirements, budget, and target platform (iOS, Android, or both). Common technology stacks include native development (Swift for iOS, Kotlin for Android) and cross-platform development (React Native, Flutter).

2. **Set Up Your Development Environment**: Prepare your development environment by installing necessary tools and software, such as Xcode for iOS, Android Studio for Android, and version control systems like Git.

3. **Backend Development**: Develop the backend of your app, which handles data storage, authentication, server-side logic, and communication with the frontend. Use frameworks like Node.js, Django, or Ruby on Rails for backend development.

4. **Frontend Development**: Develop the frontend of your app, which includes the user interface and user experience. Implement the designs using the chosen technology stack and ensure smooth interactions and performance.

5. **Integrate APIs and Services**: Integrate third-party APIs and services to enhance your app's functionality. This could include payment gateways, social media integrations, analytics, and push notifications.

6. **Testing and Debugging**: Conduct thorough testing to identify and fix bugs, performance issues, and usability problems. Use automated testing tools, unit tests, and manual testing to ensure your app is robust and reliable.

7. **App Deployment**: Deploy your app to the respective app stores (Apple App Store and Google Play Store). Follow the submission guidelines and requirements for each platform to ensure a smooth approval process.

Monetization Strategies

Monetizing your mobile app is essential for generating revenue and ensuring the sustainability of your business. Here are some popular monetization strategies:

1. **In-App Purchases**: Offer in-app purchases for additional features, content, or virtual goods. This model works well for gaming apps, freemium apps, and apps with exclusive content.

2. **Subscription Models**: Implement a subscription model where users pay a recurring fee for access to premium features or content. This model provides a steady and predictable income stream. Examples include productivity apps, streaming services, and educational apps.

3. **Advertising**: Display ads within your app using ad networks like Google AdMob, Facebook Audience Network, and MoPub. Choose between different ad formats, such as banners, interstitials, and rewarded videos, based on your app's design and user experience.

4. **Paid Apps**: Charge a one-time fee for users to download and access your app. This model is suitable for apps that offer significant value upfront and do not rely on continuous content updates or in-app purchases.

5. **Affiliate Marketing**: Partner with other businesses to promote their products or services within your app. Earn a commission for every sale or lead generated through your app. This strategy works well for niche apps with a specific target audience.

Effective Marketing Strategies

Marketing is crucial for reaching a wide audience and driving downloads for your mobile app. Here are some effective marketing strategies:

1. **App Store Optimization (ASO)**: Optimize your app's listing in the app stores to improve visibility and attract more downloads. Use relevant keywords in your app title,

description, and tags. Create an appealing app icon and screenshots to attract users.

2. **Social Media Marketing**: Leverage social media platforms to promote your app and engage with your audience. Share engaging content, run paid ads, and collaborate with influencers to reach a larger audience.

3. **Content Marketing**: Create valuable content related to your app's niche to attract and engage your target audience. This could include blog posts, videos, podcasts, and infographics. Content marketing helps build trust and authority, driving organic traffic to your app.

4. **Press and Media Coverage**: Reach out to tech blogs, industry websites, and media outlets to get coverage for your app. A press release or feature article can generate significant visibility and attract downloads.

5. **Referral Programs**: Implement a referral program where existing users can invite their friends to download your app. Offer incentives like discounts, free features, or rewards for successful referrals.

6. **Email Marketing**: Build an email list to communicate directly with your audience. Offer a lead magnet, such as a free trial or exclusive content, in exchange for email sign-ups. Send regular newsletters with updates, promotions, and valuable content to keep your audience engaged.

Post-Launch: Continuous Updates and User Feedback

Launching your app is just the beginning. Continuous updates and user feedback are crucial for maintaining and growing your app's user base and income. Here's how to manage your app post-launch:

1. **Gather User Feedback**: Encourage users to provide feedback through in-app surveys, reviews, and support channels. Use this feedback to identify areas for improvement and prioritize updates.

2. **Regular Updates**: Release regular updates to fix bugs, improve performance, and add new features. Regular updates show users that you are committed to maintaining and improving your app, enhancing user satisfaction and retention.

3. **Analyze User Data**: Use analytics tools like Google Analytics, Firebase, and Mixpanel to track user behavior, engagement, and retention. Analyze this data to make informed decisions and optimize your app's performance.

4. **Engage with Your Users**: Build a community around your app by engaging with your users on social media, forums, and support channels. Respond to their queries, address their concerns, and keep them informed about updates and new features.

5. **A/B Testing**: Conduct A/B testing to compare different versions of your app's features, design elements, and marketing strategies. Use the insights from A/B testing to optimize your app and improve user experience.

6. **Monitor Competition**: Keep an eye on your competitors and the market trends. Analyze their strategies, features, and user feedback to identify opportunities and stay ahead of the competition.

Case Studies of Successful Mobile Apps

Learning from successful mobile apps can provide valuable insights and inspiration. Here are some case studies:

1. **Fitness App**: Sarah developed a fitness app that offers personalized workout plans, nutrition tracking, and community support. By focusing on user-friendly design, regular updates, and engaging content, Sarah's app attracted a large user base. Her monetization strategy included in-app purchases for premium features and a subscription model, generating an average monthly income of $15,000.

2. **Educational App**: John created an educational app for learning languages. The app offers interactive lessons, quizzes, and real-

time feedback. John leveraged app store optimization, social media marketing, and partnerships with educational institutions to promote his app. His monetization strategy included a freemium model with in-app purchases and a subscription option. John's app generated over $20,000 per month.

3. **Productivity App**: Lisa launched a productivity app that helps users manage their tasks, set goals, and track their progress. She focused on creating a clean and intuitive design, regular updates, and responsive customer support. Lisa's marketing strategy included content marketing, email marketing, and influencer collaborations. Her app's monetization model included a one-time purchase option and a subscription for premium features, generating $10,000 monthly.

Tools and Resources for Mobile App Development

Utilizing the right tools and resources can enhance your mobile app development process. Here are some valuable tools to consider:

1. **Development Tools**: Xcode for iOS, Android Studio for Android, and cross-platform frameworks like React Native and Flutter for developing your app. These tools provide comprehensive development environments and debugging capabilities.

2. **Design Tools**: Use tools like Sketch, Figma, and Adobe XD for creating wireframes, prototypes, and user interface designs. These tools offer collaboration features and design systems to streamline the design process.

3. **Backend Services**: Utilize backend services like Firebase, AWS Amplify, and Backendless for data storage, authentication, and server-side logic. These services provide scalable and reliable backend solutions.

4. **Analytics Tools**: Google Analytics, Firebase Analytics, and Mixpanel help track user behavior, engagement, and retention. Use these tools to gather insights and optimize your app's performance.

5. **Marketing Tools**: Tools like App Annie, Sensor Tower, and MobileAction provide market intelligence, app store optimization, and competitor analysis. Email marketing platforms like Mailchimp and ConvertKit help manage your email list and campaigns.

6. **Testing Tools**: Use tools like TestFlight for iOS, Firebase Test Lab for Android, and BrowserStack for cross-platform testing. These tools help identify and fix bugs, ensuring a robust and reliable app.

Building a Sustainable Mobile App Business

Building a sustainable mobile app business requires more than just creating and launching an app. Here's how to ensure long-term success:

1. **Consistent Quality**: Maintain consistent quality in your app's design, performance, and user experience. Regularly update and improve your app to meet user expectations and industry standards.

2. **Building Relationships**: Foster strong relationships with your users. Engage with them through social media, email marketing, and personalized communication. Loyal users are more likely to make in-app purchases and recommend your app.

3. **Diversifying Income Streams**: Don't rely solely on one monetization strategy. Diversify your income streams by offering various in-app purchases, subscription models, and advertising options. Explore new features and revenue opportunities.

4. **Adapting to Changes**: Stay adaptable and be ready to pivot your strategies based on market trends and user feedback. The mobile app industry is dynamic, and staying flexible ensures continued success.

5. **Investing in Learning**: Continuously invest in learning and improving your skills. Take courses, attend webinars, and read

industry blogs to stay updated with the latest trends and best practices.

Overcoming Challenges in Mobile App Development

Developing a mobile app comes with its own set of challenges. Here's how to overcome some common obstacles:

1. **Technical Issues**: Technical issues like bugs, crashes, and performance problems can affect your app's success. Conduct thorough testing, use debugging tools, and release regular updates to address these issues.

2. **Increasing Competition**: The mobile app market is highly competitive. Differentiate your app by offering unique value, high-quality design, and exceptional user experience. Focus on building a loyal user base rather than competing solely on downloads.

3. **Monetization Struggles**: Monetizing an app can take time and effort. Experiment with different monetization strategies, track their performance, and optimize based on results. Diversify your income streams to reduce reliance on a single source.

4. **User Retention**: Retaining users can be challenging. Focus on creating engaging content, regular updates, and personalized communication to keep users coming back. Use analytics to identify and address churn points.

5. **Maintaining Motivation**: Building a successful mobile app is a long-term commitment, and maintaining motivation can be challenging. Set realistic goals, celebrate small wins, and stay focused on your long-term vision. Surround yourself with a supportive community to stay motivated.

Future Trends in Mobile App Development

Staying ahead of future trends can give you a competitive edge in the mobile app industry. Here are some trends to watch in 2024:

1. **5G Technology**: The widespread adoption of 5G technology will enhance mobile app performance, enabling faster data transfer, lower latency, and more immersive experiences. Explore opportunities to leverage 5G for your app.

2. **Artificial Intelligence (AI)**: AI-powered features like chatbots, personalized recommendations, and predictive analytics can enhance user experience and engagement. Integrate AI into your app to provide a more intelligent and personalized experience.

3. **Augmented Reality (AR) and Virtual Reality (VR)**: AR and VR technologies are transforming mobile app experiences. Incorporate AR or VR elements into your app to offer immersive and interactive experiences.

4. **Internet of Things (IoT)**: IoT integration allows mobile apps to connect and interact with smart devices. Explore opportunities to create apps that control or monitor IoT devices, enhancing convenience and functionality.

5. **Blockchain Technology**: Blockchain technology offers secure and transparent transactions, data storage, and authentication. Consider integrating blockchain for enhanced security and trust in your app.

Developing mobile apps offers powerful opportunities to reach millions of users, generate significant income, and make a positive impact.

By validating your app idea, designing a user-friendly interface, developing the app using appropriate technologies, and implementing effective monetization and marketing strategies, you can build a successful and sustainable mobile app business. Continuous updates, user feedback, and staying current with industry trends are crucial for long-term success.

My journey in mobile app development has shown that with dedication and the right approach, achieving significant income and making a positive impact is entirely possible. I took ideas I had, and found a developer I can trust, where he helped me create a few products with software . These you can find on my limitlesspassionltd.com site where I use each software I created, based on my ideas, to help anyone get started online.

Conclusion and Next Steps

Achieving and exceeding your goal of earning $1,000 per month requires innovation, persistence, and adaptability. By applying the strategies and insights discussed throughout this book, you can build a solid foundation for financial success.

Reflecting on the Journey

Since starting my online business in 2012, I've experienced the highs and lows of entrepreneurship. I built my business from scratch, covering all the subjects discussed in this book, and I can confidently say that the journey is both challenging and incredibly rewarding. Take it from someone who has walked the walk—financial independence is attainable with dedication, strategic planning, and continuous learning.

Reviewing and Refining Your Strategies

Continuous improvement is crucial for long-term success. Regularly review and refine your strategies to ensure they remain effective and aligned with your goals. Here's how to approach this:

1. **Analyze Performance**: Use analytics tools to track the performance of your ventures. Identify what's working and what's not, and make data-driven decisions to optimize your strategies.

2. **Gather Feedback**: Solicit feedback from your audience, customers, and peers. Constructive feedback can provide valuable insights and highlight areas for improvement.

3. **Stay Agile**: Be open to change and ready to pivot your strategies based on market trends and new opportunities. Staying agile allows you to adapt quickly and stay ahead of the competition.

Scaling Your Ventures

Scaling your business is essential for increasing your income and achieving your financial goals. Here are some steps to scale your ventures effectively:

1. **Automate Tasks**: Leverage technology to automate repetitive tasks, such as email marketing, social media posting, and customer support. Automation saves time and allows you to focus on strategic growth.

2. **Expand Your Reach**: Explore new markets, niches, and platforms to expand your reach. International markets, new product lines, and additional sales channels can drive growth.

3. **Build a Team**: As your business grows, consider hiring additional staff or freelancers to manage tasks and support your operations. Building a capable team enables you to scale without becoming overwhelmed.

Continuously Upgrading Your Skills

Investing in your personal and professional development is vital for staying competitive and innovative. Here's how to continuously upgrade your skills:

1. **Take Courses**: Enroll in online courses, attend workshops, and participate in webinars to learn new skills and stay updated with industry trends. Platforms like Udemy, Coursera, and LinkedIn Learning offer valuable resources.

2. **Read and Research**: Stay informed by reading industry blogs, books, and research papers. Continuous learning keeps you ahead of the curve and inspires new ideas.

3. **Network and Collaborate**: Connect with other professionals, join industry groups, and attend conferences. Networking can lead to collaborations, partnerships, and new opportunities.

Diversifying Your Income Streams

Relying on a single income source can be risky. Diversify your income streams to reduce risk and increase financial stability. Here's how:

1. **Explore Multiple Ventures**: Don't limit yourself to one business model. Explore various ventures, such as affiliate marketing, e-commerce, online courses, and real estate crowdfunding.

2. **Invest in Passive Income**: Look for opportunities to generate passive income, such as dividend investing, rental properties, and digital products. Passive income provides financial security and frees up time for other pursuits.

3. **Reinvest Profits**: Reinvest a portion of your profits into new ventures, marketing, and skill development. Reinvestment fuels growth and helps you achieve your long-term financial goals.

Leveraging Technology

Technology can significantly enhance your business operations and efficiency. Here's how to leverage technology effectively:

1. **Use Advanced Tools**: Invest in advanced tools and software for analytics, marketing, project management, and customer relationship management (CRM). These tools streamline operations and improve decision-making.

2. **Implement AI and Automation**: Explore AI-powered solutions and automation tools to enhance productivity and scalability. AI can provide insights, automate tasks, and improve customer interactions.

3. **Stay Updated**: Keep abreast of technological advancements and trends. Incorporating new technologies can give you a competitive edge and open up new opportunities.

Expanding Your Network

Building a strong network is crucial for accessing new opportunities and gaining support. Here's how to expand your network:

1. **Attend Events**: Participate in industry conferences, seminars, and networking events. These gatherings provide opportunities to meet like-minded professionals and potential partners.

2. **Join Online Communities**: Engage with online communities and forums related to your industry. Contributing to discussions and sharing your expertise can build your reputation and attract valuable connections.

3. **Mentorship and Collaboration**: Seek mentorship from experienced professionals and offer mentorship to others. Collaborate with peers on projects, joint ventures, and cross-promotions to expand your reach and influence.

Staying Informed and Proactive

The business landscape is constantly evolving, and staying informed is essential for staying competitive. Here's how to remain proactive:

1. **Monitor Trends**: Keep an eye on industry trends, market shifts, and emerging technologies. Staying informed helps you anticipate changes and adapt your strategies accordingly.

2. **Regularly Review Goals**: Regularly review and adjust your goals based on your progress and changing circumstances. Setting and achieving short-term goals keeps you motivated and on track.

3. **Seek Opportunities**: Be proactive in seeking new opportunities for growth and innovation. Whether it's exploring a new market, launching a new product, or collaborating with others, always be on the lookout for ways to expand.

Commitment to Your Financial Independence Journey

Achieving financial independence requires dedication, strategic planning, and a commitment to continuous improvement. Here's how to stay committed to your journey:

1. **Set Clear Goals**: Define clear, achievable financial goals and create a roadmap to reach them. Break down your goals into actionable steps and track your progress.

2. **Stay Motivated**: Keep your motivation high by celebrating milestones, visualizing your success, and staying focused on your long-term vision. Surround yourself with a supportive network that encourages and inspires you.

3. **Adapt and Overcome**: Embrace challenges and setbacks as opportunities to learn and grow. Stay resilient and adaptable, and be willing to pivot your strategies when necessary.

Final Thoughts

Since starting my online business in 2012, I've built a successful venture from scratch, covering all the subjects discussed in this book. My journey has been filled with challenges, learning experiences, and achievements, and I can confidently say that financial independence is within your reach.

By reviewing and refining your strategies, scaling your ventures, continuously upgrading your skills, and leveraging technology, you can surpass your financial goals.

Diversify your income streams, reinvest your profits, and expand your network to unlock new opportunities. Stay informed, proactive, and committed to your financial independence journey.